D1532409

DANETTE J. CRAWFORD

*A 45-Day Encounter with God
that Changes Everything*

BREAK
Free

BREAK FREE
A 45-Day Encounter with God that Changes Everything

Danette Joy Crawford
P.O. Box 65036 • Virginia Beach, VA 23467
www.DanetteCrawford.com

ISBN: 978-1-64123-554-9 • eBook ISBN: 978-1-64123-555-6
Printed in the United States of America
© 2020 by Danette Joy Crawford

Whitaker House
1030 Hunt Valley Circle • New Kensington, PA 15068
www.whitakerhouse.com

Library of Congress Cataloging-in-Publication Data (Pending)

1 2 3 4 5 6 7 8 9 10 11 ⅃⅃ 27 26 25 24 23 22 21 20

DEDICATION

This book is dedicated to my brother, Denny. I love you so very much! You have a sensitive, caring heart for others, and I'm blessed to have you as a brother. John 8:36 says, *"So if the Son sets you free, you will be free indeed."* As you have personally experienced in your life, Jesus is the only one who can heal, deliver, and enable us to *Break Free* from everything that the enemy tries to entangle us with. I love you and I'm proud of you!

CONTENTS

INTRODUCTION: THE ONLY WAY OUT OF ANY PIT

Everyone who calls on the name of
the Lord will be saved.
—Romans 10:13

Maybe, today, you feel like I felt years ago—suffering so much emotional brokenness that I didn't know which end was up. Maybe you've dealt with betrayal, defeat, physical illness, emotional anguish, or any number of pits in which you've felt trapped, without hope of rescue. If that's the case, I want to tell you that there is a way out of every pit—in fact, the *only* Way. His name is Jesus Christ, and He is the only One capable of rescuing anyone out of every possible pit. Maybe you have thought about God, but have never taken that step to accept Him into your life as your personal Savior. As a child, I prayed every night, but I didn't pray a prayer of salvation and accept Christ as my Savior until I was seventeen years old.

I can tell you confidently that it was Jesus Christ alone who got me out of my pit—a pit of sin a nd emotional broken-ness. The Bible tells us that we have *all* sinned and fallen short of God's glory. (See Romans 3:23.) Yet God loved us so much that He gave His only Son, Jesus, to die on the cross for us, so we could be forgiven of our sins. *"For God so loved the world that he gave his one and only Son, that whoever believes in him shall not perish but have eternal life"* (John 3:16).

For us to accept this awesome gift of salvation, we simply have to follow the steps outlined in Romans 10:9–10:

> *If you declare with your mouth, "Jesus is Lord," and believe in your heart that God raised him from the dead, you will be saved. For it is with your heart that you believe and are justified, and it is with your mouth that you profess your faith and are saved.*

1. We must confess with our mouths that we are sinners and that Jesus is Lord.

2. We must believe in our hearts that Jesus is the Son of God, and that God raised Him from the dead.

I want to invite you to accept Christ into your life as your Savior by saying this simple prayer:

> Dear Jesus, I believe that You are the Son of God, and that You died on the cross for me and rose again so that I can be forgiven for my sins. I confess to You this day that I am a sinner. Please forgive me of my sins and come into my heart right now as my Lord and Savior. Amen.

If you prayed that prayer, I want to congratulate you for making the most important decision you will ever make—and for grabbing the strongest rope of hope available to get you out of the pit! I also want to welcome you to the family of God. Make sure you tell as many people as you can that you are now a Christian!

Are you looking up from a dark pit with high walls and no ladder in sight? If so, I want to extend a rope of hope to you! Your situation may seem hopeless. Your pain may be overwhelming. Yet there is Someone who knows your sorrows even better than you do, and He will bring you out of your pit. Even in your pit, you're not alone; the Lord is with you, no matter how deep and dark it may be.

PITS ARE PROBABLE BUT NOT NECESSARILY PERMANENT

*Many are the afflictions of the righteous, but the LORD
delivers him out of them all.*
—Psalm 34:19 NKJV

If you feel as if you're in a pit, remember that you're not the first person to find yourself looking up from within what feels like a deep, dark hole. And you're in good company, too. Proverbial *pits* are situations common to all people—male and female, rich and poor, young and old. They were also a common complaint of just about every biblical character... at least the ones we strive to be like. From Adam and Eve to Joseph to the apostle Paul, our Christian brothers and sisters became famous *because of* the pits from which the Lord delivered them!

In the Old Testament, we read about Joseph, who found himself in a literal pit that turned into a decades-long slump during which his name, his reputation, and his integrity were dragged in the dirt. (See Genesis 37:5–36; 39; 41:14–44.)

For Joseph, that pit looked like a dark dead end, but it was truly a pathway to the palace—a direct route at that, so much so that in the end, he could say to the people who had put him in a pit in the first place, *"You intended to harm me, but God intended it for good to accomplish what is now being done, the saving of many lives"* (Genesis 50:20).

In the New Testament, we read about the apostle Paul, a respected Jewish leader who became a Christian, won souls for Jesus, and consequently found himself in his own pit. Paul's pit was in the form of a ship tossed in a raging storm. Everybody wanted to jump off the boat, but God told Paul, "Don't abandon ship—you'll come through this!" (See Acts 27.)

If you're feeling trapped today, I want to encourage you— don't abandon ship! Yes, your pit may seem overwhelming. Yes, you may be in the midst of the biggest storm of your life. But I can promise you, it's temporary. When you trust your Father God and obey Him, He will guide you out of the pit. This, too, shall pass.

Both Joseph and Paul needed a rope of hope to climb out of the pit. That rope was the same one that's available for you: God's Word. The Bible provides a map to guide us out of any and every pit that we find ourselves in. Our memory verse for today is Psalm 34:19, *"Many are the afflictions of the righteous, but the LORD delivers him out of them all"* (NKJV). In other words, we all will experience *pits* in our lives—they're inevitable—but we can escape when we grab hold of the rope of hope and determine to climb out.

REFLECTION

1. Thinking about the pits you've experienced, how would you classify them? Check all that apply.

___ Physical (health-related)

___ Emotional

___ Mental

___ Financial

___ Relational

___ Spiritual

___ Other: _____

2. What encouragement can you take from Psalm 34:19?

3. In seeking escape from your pit(s), where have you looked for rescue? List all the resources you've called upon, paying attention to whether you've looked to God and His Word, and to what degree.

_____

_____

_____

Declaration

God has promised to deliver me from my pits if I'll only trust in Him.

SOME PITS
ARE SELF-IMPOSED

Above all else, guard your heart,
for everything you do flows from it.
—Proverbs 4:23

M any times, words are what put us in a pit—words
spoken to us, about us, or even by us. The Bible rightly says
that the power of life and death is in our tongues. (See Proverbs
18:21.) When words that don't align with the Word of truth
are spoken, we can quickly find ourselves in a pit dug by the
power of those words. It is important not to allow anyone
to speak negative words over you, and not to speak negative
words over yourself.

I'm in no way blaming you for any pits you might find
yourself stuck in today. I'd only like to ask you to consider
closely what you say, what you listen to, and what you believe.
Some pits can be avoided if we only guard our hearts and
minds against falsehood by renewing them in the truth of
God's Word, as Romans 12:2 teaches us. When we live surrendered to God's Holy Spirit and allow Him to guide our

paths, we end up sidestepping so many pits that we otherwise would have fallen into.

For the first seventeen years of my life, I lived according to the dictates of my soul—my will, emotions, natural mind, and fleshly desires. In other words, what I wanted, what I thought, and how I felt. After I accepted Christ as my Lord and Savior, the Holy Spirit began teaching me to yield to my renewed spirit, which needed to be under the Spirit's control. I like to call this surrender *soul control*. And mastering soul control takes a lifetime. Even when we feel that we generally cede to the Holy Spirit's leading, we find ourselves facing situations in which our souls are not under the control of our renewed spirits. In these cases, it becomes all about what we want, what we think, and how we feel.

Our spirits desire to act righteously and do the will of the Father; they long for fellowship with the Lord. But getting our souls and our flesh in agreement with our spirits takes some effort. Our spirits want to forgive and walk in love, but our natural minds interrupt and say, *Forgive her? You must be crazy. Don't you remember what she did to you? You have a right to be angry.* Then, our emotions jump in and remind us just how we felt. Rejected. Unloved. Left out. In the soul realm, it's all about self. But when we die to self and follow Christ, it's no longer about self; it's about Christ.

When we get our minds, wills, and emotions in line with our spirits that are led by the Holy Spirit, nothing can stop us from experiencing the Lord's blessings in abundance. When we practice soul control, we find ourselves falling into fewer pits of our own making. The things that would have tripped us up when we were governed by our soul no longer have power over us. The petty problems and pride-based offenses that might have harmed us beyond recovery are now easily brushed off by our understanding of who we are in Christ.

As we maintain soul control, we can be led by the Holy Spirit. The Holy Spirit will fill us and guide us into all truth— truth about how to handle every situation and truth about our own hearts' conditions. And that's a sure way to stay out of a lot of life's pits.

REFLECTION

1. Describe the concept of "soul control" in your own words.

_____

_____

_____

_____

2. The following are a set of possible scenarios you might encounter. For each one, first jot down what your response would be if you were controlled by your soul, and then write out a different response if you were using soul control. I've included an example to help get you started.

Someone cuts you off in traffic.

Soul response: Anger; gesturing rudely or shouting obscenities; tailgating

Soul control response: Taking a deep breath and praying for the safety of the driver; telling yourself that he or she probably needed to be somewhere in a hurry and choosing to release him or her to God

Your spouse forgets your birthday.

Soul response: _____

_____

_____

Soul control response: _____

_____

_____

You are passed over for a promotion that's given instead to someone who doesn't work as hard or demonstrate as much integrity as you.

Soul response: _____

_____

_____

Soul control response: _____

_____

_____

At a restaurant, your server brings you a meal that is under-cooked and unappealing.

Soul response: _____

_____

_____

Soul control response: _____

_____

_____

Declaration

I will live according to the leading of the Holy Spirit,
giving Him control of my spirit and soul.

ESCAPE THE PIT OF REJECTION

Though my father and mother forsake me,
the LORD will receive me.
—Psalm 27:10

Growing up, one of my greatest unmet needs was to feel accepted. We had a tumultuous home environment, and even my parents' divorce did not settle matters much. My brothers and I handled our home situation in different ways, my strategy being to strive for irreproachability and overall perfection. As a result, I placed unrealistic expectations on myself in every area.

My low self-esteem and thoughts of worthlessness were hidden successfully behind my many accomplishments. I earned numerous academic awards, graduated with high honors, and held a job as a teenager to assist my mom with mounting financial needs. All of these pursuits masked my emotional pain, blinding me to the fact that I was desperate to feel loved and accepted.

The loss of a parent through divorce or death is just one of many ways by which a spirit of rejection can build a stronghold in our lives. The spirit of rejection was the greatest stronghold the enemy strategically built in my life as a child. *Strongholds* are arguments and pretensions Satan presents to us that contradict the Word of God. Satan pretends they are truth, and he can put forth some very convincing arguments. However, the Word of God is the ultimate source of truth about everything, including our identity in Christ. And Christ has given us the weapons with which to wage a successful fight against the devil and demolish his every stronghold.

The Word of God, also called the *"sword of the Spirit"* (Ephesians 6:17), and the fruit of the Spirit—*"love, joy, peace, patience, kindness, goodness, faithfulness, gentleness and self-control"* (Galatians 5:22–23)—have divine power to demolish Satan's strongholds.

When the devil was establishing a stronghold of rejection in my young life, I lived in that pit of rejection. It was not until a few years after I gave my life to the Lord that I began to practice saying out loud, "I'm not rejected—I'm accepted! I am accepted by Christ." As we speak the Word of truth, we renew our minds. Out with the old lies and in with the truth!

The devil wants us to be susceptible to rejection, but the Lord wants us to be rejection proof. Society may reject us if we don't look a certain way, act a certain way, or earn a certain income. Society tries to teach our children at an early age to reject those who don't wear brand-name clothes or who don't have the same color skin or who don't speak with the same accent. We need to be rejection proof more than ever so that we can walk boldly with the Lord before an increasingly god-less society.

Although other people may really reject us for various reasons throughout our lives, God never rejects us. Again, He tells us, *"I have chosen you and have not rejected you"* (Isaiah 41:9).

Keeping this in mind, we can have a clear perspective when faced with rejection. If others reject us, we can know that their negative words or actions don't define who we are. Most of the time, those words and actions actually define who *they* are.

Is there someone who always speaks negatively to you and about you? Most likely, that person's words actually reflect his or her own hurt. Rejection is a tactic people often use in an effort to control and manipulate others' actions, choices, and behaviors. Those who reject you may not even be aware that their underlying motive is to control you; yet it's only when you do what they want, when and how they want it, that they withdraw their rejection and give you their stamp of approval. Whatever the case, it's highly probable that those who reject you have experienced a great deal of rejection themselves, and have never learned healthy ways of relating to others. Keeping this perspective in mind may lessen the sting of rejection when you feel it and enable you to invoke the healing balm of empathy.

It's also important to remember that nothing anyone else may think or say can undermine your worth to God. When you know who you are in Christ, receive the unconditional love

God has for you, and acknowledge God's acceptance, you'll become rejection proof. You have to know it in your heart and in your spirit, not just in your mind. This knowledge comes only when you regularly study and meditate on God's Word and spend time in His presence through prayer and worship.

REFLECTION

1. Do you have any idea just how much God loves you? How precious you are to Him? Read through the following passages and summarize the implications of what they say about the way God views you.

> *God demonstrates his own love for us in this: While we were still sinners, Christ died for us.*   (Romans 5:8)

_____

_____

_____

> *"For I know the plans I have for you," declares the LORD, "plans to prosper you and not to harm you, plans to give you hope and a future."*   (Jeremiah 29:11)

_____

_____

_____

Are not two sparrows sold for a penny? Yet not one of them will fall to the ground outside your Father's care. And even the very hairs of your head are all numbered. So don't be afraid; you are worth more than many sparrows. (Matthew 10:29–31)

_____

_____

_____

2. Have you struggled with feelings of rejection from a person or a group or people? Or maybe even from God? If so, list the person or group of people here:

_____

_____

3. What kinds of emotions crop up when you think about this person or group of people? What have they led you to believe, or tried to lead you to believe, about yourself?

4. I would like to lead you in a prayer of release from the sense of rejection you have been experiencing.

Heavenly Father, You know how I struggle with feeling rejected by _____. I acknowledge that Your view of me is the only one that really matters, and I ask You to help me to prize Your opinion of me above all others. Help me to understand just how special and valuable I am to You as Your son/daughter, and enable me to walk in freedom from the spirit of rejection as I dwell in the glorious joy of Your love. In Jesus's name, amen.

Declaration

No matter how others view me, God loves me immensely and treasures me immeasurably.

RECOGNIZE PERCEIVED REJECTION

The fear of human opinion disables;
trusting in God protects you from that.
—Proverbs 29:25 MSG

I worked with a young lady who became very defensive if anyone corrected her, however gently. Sensing that her reactions stemmed from a root of rejection, I talked to her about it and learned that, as a sixteen-year-old, she had lost her mother to illness, only to have her father leave home shortly thereafter to live with a new girlfriend for two months. The girlfriend ultimately moved in with the family, and my coworker's father married her on the one-year anniversary of his wife's death. His daughter felt a double sting, dealing with a sense of rejection of both herself and her mother, and she began to interpret many routine interactions as further personal rejection. For example, if an office meeting occurred without her being included, even if the meeting agenda didn't concern her work, she would feel rejected, taking the exclusion personally. And even when she'd been invited to participate in a meeting or activity, she often felt excluded. This woman was truly deceived by her perceptions of the way others treated her.

Today, as a result of God's grace and love, she has overcome the stronghold of rejection. The recovery process required her to acknowledge her issue and allow the Holy Spirit to change her biased perceptions. Now, she serves as a vital member of my staff, and God is using her to minister to others dealing with issues of rejection.

There are two types of rejection: actual rejection and perceived rejection. Both can hurt if we haven't been made *rejection proof* by our heavenly Father. Perceived rejection is a device of the devil, of whom the Bible says, "*He was a murderer from the beginning, not holding to the truth, for there is no truth in him. When he lies, he speaks his native language, for he is a liar and the father of lies*" (John 8:44). The devil is delighted when we feel rejected; if he can't send actual rejection our way, he'll attempt to mess with our perceptions. Through *perception deception*, he deceives us into thinking that other people have rejected us.

Unless we have an intimate relationship with Christ, any rejection we experience, whether real or perceived, will produce fear within us—and accompanying feelings of discouragement, self-doubt, and dismay. But 2 Timothy 1:7 reassures us that "*God has not given us a spirit of fear, but of power and of love and of a sound mind*" (NKJV). We must be led by the Holy Spirit, not controlled by other people and their perceived opinions of us. The Word says that the fear of man—which includes the fear of rejection—will entrap us. The Word of

God tells us, *"Fear of man will prove to be a snare, but whoever trusts in the* LORD *is kept safe"* (Proverbs 29:25). The devil
wants us to perceive rejection that isn't really there. Don't fall
for his schemes! Remember, you are a beloved child of the
King of Kings, and His opinion is all that matters.

REFLECTION

1. Describe, in your own words, the difference between
perceived rejection and *actual rejection.*

_____

_____

_____

2. Think about some instances when you felt rejected. In
the space below, describe those instances briefly, and circle the
corresponding type of rejection you believe you were experiencing—either actual or perceived.

Instance of rejection

_____   *Actual   Perceived*

_____   *Actual   Perceived*

_____   *Actual   Perceived*

_____   *Actual   Perceived*

_____   *Actual   Perceived*

3. Were you surprised by any of your above categorizations of instances of feeling rejected? Has God opened your mind to any new realizations regarding those experiences? If so, record your thoughts here.

_____

_____

_____

Declaration

*I won't jump to conclusions in interpreting others'
perceptions of me but will cling above all to
God's high opinion of me.*

FORGIVENESS SETS US FREE

*Bear with each other and forgive one another if
any of you has a grievance against someone.
Forgive as the Lord forgave you.*
—Colossians 3:13

When we find ourselves wounded because of a broken relationship, we must realize that the first step toward healing is to examine our own hearts. It's easy to point the finger and judge others, but we all must answer to the Lord regarding our own hearts. Maybe we were rejected, abandoned, or abused by someone. No matter what we've been through at the hands of others, we must release those people and forgive them if we truly desire healing.

If we refuse to release those who have harmed us and caused us pain, we only prolong our suffering. It has been medically proven that many health problems, including certain types of cancer, can result from such toxic emotions as anger, hatred, bitterness, unforgiveness, and anxiety. Unhealthy emotions not only cripple us spiritually, they also can destroy us physically.

Worse still, if we fail to forgive others for the wrongs they've done to us, we can't expect to experience forgiveness from God—definitely not a blessing we want to forfeit! Jesus said, *"If you forgive other people when they sin against you, your heavenly Father will also forgive you"* (Matthew 6:14). On the heels of that wonderful promise, He gave us this warning: *"But if you do not forgive others their sins, your Father will not forgive your sins"* (Matthew 6:15).

The first step in the process of forgiving someone is to acknowledge that you've been hurt. Many Christian believers try to repress their emotional, mental, and physical wounds by covering them with a big, spiritual Band-Aid, singing a little louder in worship and jumping a little higher in praise to mask their hurt feelings. Yet a smiling face on the outside can't hide an offense festering on the inside for very long.

The second step is to take your hurt and to lay it at the foot of the cross of Jesus as you say, "Lord, I forgive that person for hurting me. I release him or her from everything they have done to hurt me. I choose to forgive. As You have forgiven me of my sins, Lord, I forgive them for their sins against me. Amen." By humbling yourself and praying this prayer of forgiveness, you are released from the oppression that unforgiveness puts on your heart. Once you forgive, you will feel as though the weight of the world has been lifted off your shoulders.

The third step of forgiveness is refusing to entertain negative thoughts about the person or people who hurt you. It is your responsibility to *"take captive every thought to make it obedient to Christ"* (2 Corinthians 10:5). Don't allow yourself to rehearse or rehash an offense. Your struggle is not against flesh and blood (the person or people who hurt you)—it's against the spiritual forces of evil in the heavenly realms. (See Ephesians 6:12.) When you look at or think about your offenders, stop focusing on the bad and start looking instead with eyes of love for the good.

The fourth step is to pray for your offenders. Jesus said, *"Love your enemies and pray for those who persecute you"* (Matthew 5:44). Pray that God would do for your enemies what you would want Him to do for you. Follow these instructions of the apostle Peter: *"Above all, love each other deeply, because love covers over a multitude of sins"* (1 Peter 4:8).

A final step to seal the process of forgiveness is to seek reconciliation with your offenders, if that seems a wise course of action. Ask the Lord for wisdom on how to talk to and communicate openly with those who have offended you. If a conversation occurs, don't verbally attack but only communicate your feelings honestly and calmly, then express forgiveness and seek reconciliation.

Are you struggling with unforgiveness today? *"Do not let the sun go down while you are still angry, and do not give the devil a foothold"* (Ephesians 4:26–27). In other words, don't give the devil an access point to your life by refusing to forgive! Allow the Holy Spirit to search your heart today, and then extend forgiveness to anyone against whom you've been harboring bitterness and resentment.

REFLECTION

1. Why is it important to forgive and release those who have hurt and wounded us?

_____

_____

_____

2. Whom do you need to release and forgive today?

_____

_____

_____

3. When you're ready, write out a prayer in which you express forgiveness of that person or persons and also petition God to bless his or her life.

_____

_____

_____

Declaration

Because I stand forgiven by the King of Kings, I can extend forgiveness to those who hurt me.

AVOID THE SNARE OF REVENGE

*Do not repay evil with evil or insult with insult. On the
contrary, repay evil with blessing, because to this you
were called so that you may inherit a blessing.*
—1 Peter 3:9

The opposite of forgiving someone who has wronged you
is retaliating or seeking revenge. But we must never respond
to the sins that others commit against us by committing sin
ourselves. Only God and His presence can ultimately satisfy
us. Sin never satisfies in the long run. It may feel good in the
moment, but if you cultivate the seeds of sin, they will grow to
maturity, and full-grown sin gives birth to spiritual death—
and possibly even physical death.

One person who understood this truth and perfectly
embodied forgiveness, though he had every right to harbor
a vengeful attitude, was Joseph. His own brothers, jealous
of the favoritism their father showed Joseph, plotted to kill
him, but instead sold him off to a band of nomads. Joseph
ended up as a slave in the palace of Pharaoh, where he

ultimately worked his way up to being one of the top advisers to Potiphar, the captain of the guard—until a wrongful accusation by Potiphar's wife landed him in prison. It would be years until Joseph proved his integrity and found himself in a role of leadership—a role that would eventually give him the perfect chance to exact revenge on his brothers. (See Genesis 37, 39–43.) But did Joseph ever call out anyone who'd wronged him? Did he give his wicked brothers what they deserved?

Amazingly, Joseph exhibited great self-restraint and bravely put up with these injustices against him. And how did he do this? I believe it was due, at least in part, to the fact that Joseph knew God was in charge, working all things together for his good, as he explained to his brothers in Genesis 50:20. The Bible says it was obvious that God was with Joseph; God *"gave him success in everything he did"* (Genesis 39:3). And we see in Joseph's response to Potiphar's wife when she tried to seduce him (see Genesis 39:9) that he was committed to serving God faithfully and not sinning. Joseph would rather put up with injustice and remain faithful to God than sinfully betray or get back at another. Because Joseph trusted God completely, he was able to withstand the temptation to retaliate and instead sit back and wait for God to work. And work God did, ultimately promoting Joseph to the highest position of authority in Egypt.

God will do the same for us if we keep our hearts right. Maybe God is working on your behalf but you can't see it right now. Even if the enemy is trying to steal, kill, and destroy in your life, the promise of God to you is that your Father will work all things together for your good—if only you keep your heart right and refuse to seek revenge.

REFLECTION

1. Read Genesis chapters 37 and 39 through 45 to get a full picture of the experiences of Joseph as he journeyed, literally, from a pit to a prison to a palace. How did God bring blessing out of Joseph's pain?

_____

_____

_____

2. Have you ever been hurt or wronged in such a way that God brought about a blessing afterward? Explain.

_____

_____

_____

3. Think about a time when you retaliated against someone who had wronged you. What was the result? How might you have acted to extend forgiveness instead, and how might

the results have been different? Just so you know, it isn't too late to extend forgiveness!

_____

_____

_____

Declaration

God has the power to turn my pains into promotions.

DISMANTLING EMOTIONAL WALLS

A man who isolates himself seeks his own desire; he rages against all wise judgment.
—Proverbs 18:1 NKJV

Sometimes, our reaction to wrongs and rejection isn't seeking revenge but rather seeking to isolate ourselves, building emotional walls around our hearts that we believe will protect us from all future hurt. The biggest problem with putting up walls is that no one can get in—including those who really love us and care about us, those with whom being in relationship is life-giving. While emotional walls may temporarily prevent us from getting hurt, they also isolate us in a world of loneliness.

The Lord is the only One who can enable us to endure rejection, ridicule, and other emotionally painful experiences. And, by the wisdom of His Holy Spirit, He will teach us how to build healthy boundaries, not walls. We need to have healthy boundaries, and we need to keep our guards up; however, we're not to live in isolation behind self-erected walls.

First Corinthians 16:13 tells us, *"Be on your guard; stand firm in the faith; be courageous; be strong."* We must be on guard, for our enemy *"prowls around like a roaring lion looking for someone to devour"* (1 Peter 5:8). We must stay on guard in prayer and keep up our defenses by being aware of the enemy's schemes, but we must take down any isolating walls we've built because emotional walls are a carnal attempt to keep ourselves from getting hurt again.

Hurts are guaranteed this side of heaven. Jesus even told His disciples to expect persecution and other forms of suffering at the hands of others. (See, for example, John 15:18–20.) Although I can't promise you'll never get hurt again, I can promise you that building *walls* is not the way to go.

Another tactic that isolates us is to blame others for our misfortunes. The nature of our flesh is to blame someone else when we experience undesirable circumstances. If you suddenly stub your toe while walking around the house, it's likely that you'll immediately yell and want to blame whoever is nearby. One time, while sitting in a brand-new car, I spilled a 42-ounce drink all over the floor. I immediately started yelling at the person in the passenger seat. The spill wasn't her fault, of course, but my flesh immediately sought someone else to blame and decided on her. As far as the flesh goes, things haven't changed that much since the garden of Eden, where Adam blamed Eve, and Eve blamed the serpent. Sound familiar?

In many cases, when we blame others, we're secretly angry at ourselves and just don't want to own up to our mistakes. But we are not to look for someone else to be the scapegoat for the troubles we face. Instead, we are to search our own hearts and put our trust in the Lord, as Psalm 4:4–5 exhorts us.

When we're in a pit of pain and anger, whether directed at ourselves or at others, we must take our anger to the cross for the Holy Spirit to deal with it. As we lay our brokenness before the Lord, the Holy Spirit will heal us and set us free. All we need to do is cry out to the Lord and choose to release those who have hurt and wounded us by forgiving them.

REFLECTION

1. Putting up a wall is a common defense mechanism when we're feeling hurt or rejected. Why is this tactic ineffective and even potentially harmful?

_____

_____

_____

2. Think about a situation or a person that has caused you to build a wall around yourself. Confess that wall to God and pray for His Holy Spirit to dismantle it by His power.

_____

_____

_____

3. Why do we tend to place blame on others, even in situations for which no person or thing can be identified as responsible? Pay attention to the times when you search for a scapegoat, and turn those situations over to God in prayer instead.

_____

_____

_____

Declaration

In Christ, I'm free to love and be loved without fear of hurt or need to blame.

UPROOTING
UNRIGHTEOUS ANGER

*Everyone should be quick to listen, slow to speak and
slow to become angry, because human anger does not
produce the righteousness that God desires.*
—James 1:19–20

I am eternally grateful to God for the special friends who
have *loved down* my walls at various times. I'm also thankful
that He showed me the extent of my anger when, in my early
twenties, I was consumed by that emotion. Anger, in itself, can
be a sort of wall we erect that colors our view of the world and
also keeps others from penetrating our sphere of existence,
even those whose loving presence could be an immeasurable
blessing.

Of course, it's natural to feel angry whenever we feel
rejected, slighted, unvalued, or maligned. Anger is a God-
given emotion that rises up within us when we have been
mistreated, when we see others being mistreated, and when
we encounter other forms of injustice. The Bible tells us, *"Be
angry, and do not sin"* (Ephesians 4:26 NKJV). From this verse,

we know that it isn't wrong to be angry, but it *is* wrong to sin within the context of anger.

Although we can be angry and not sin, the Word tells us numerous times to be slow to anger, just as the Lord is. *"The Lord is gracious and compassionate, slow to anger and rich in love"* (Psalm 145:8). Most of the time, we are the opposite—quick to anger and slow to love—and that isn't the way God desires for us to live.

When we have a root of anger in our lives, we tend to fly off the handle at every little thing that annoys us. A root of anger will cause us to live in constant frustration and inner turmoil; we will erupt like volcanoes, spew angry words, and exhibit other destructive behaviors. Yet none of this brings about the righteousness of Christ in our lives.

We must heed the apostle Paul's instructions in Ephesians 4:26–27: *"'In your anger do not sin': Do not let the sun go down while you are still angry, and do not give the devil a foothold."* Paul was saying, in effect, that it's all right to become angry as long as you don't *stay* angry. By the end of the day, we must release the person who has angered us by forgiving him or her, because any anger that we allow to linger in our hearts can give the devil a foothold in our lives. No matter what someone has done to hurt you, it's never worth it to hang on to your anger, nor is it pleasing to the Lord.

Every night, we should ask the Holy Spirit to search our hearts, fulfilling the command of Psalm 4:4. If we allow Him to so, the Holy Spirit will show us any offenses we have picked up and any wrong heart attitudes we have exhibited throughout the day. After we ask the Holy Spirit to reveal these things to us, we need to be silent before the Lord and wait for Him to speak to us. Too often, we do all the talking, and we don't take the time to listen to what the Lord wants to say to us. As we learn to be silent, the Holy Spirit will reveal the will of the Father to us.

Today, choose to release your anger and forgive all those who have hurt and rejected you. You can become the very thing you hate if you don't forgive. Forgive others as your Father has forgiven you. (See Ephesians 4:32.) Call on the name of the Lord and allow Him to shower you with His love. He wants you to overcome and to make you rejection proof, but you first have to lay your pain and anger at His feet.

REFLECTION

1. Reflecting on Psalm 4:4 and Ephesians 4:26, explain how it is possible to be angry and yet not sin.

_____

_____

_____

2. Think about some of the things that make you angry, then classify your anger as *righteous* or *unrighteous*. I've included a few examples to get you started.

human trafficking	righteous
my spouse's snoring	unrighteous

3. Now, go to God in prayer about some of those things that cause you to experience unrighteous anger. See if you can release any of them to Him.

Declaration

Anger has no hold on me because I've been set free to love by the love of Christ.

WALK IN LOVE

You have heard that it was said, "Love your neighbor and hate your enemy." But I tell you, love your enemies and pray for those who persecute you, that you may be children of your Father in heaven.
—Matthew 5:43–45

We've talked about the importance of learning to control our anger and to surrender our vengeful urges over to the Lord. But He expects us to do a lot more than merely withhold anger from those who offend us. That's right—He expects us to love our enemies. He asks, *"If all you do is love the lovable, do you expect a bonus? Anybody can do that. If you simply say hello to those who greet you, do you expect a medal? Any run-of-the-mill sinner does that"* (Matthew 5:46–47 MSG). Loving our enemies is perhaps one of the most challenging charges Jesus gave to us, His followers. And yet it's not just a suggestion or a helpful guideline—it's a requirement.

In our relationships with other people, there's nothing more important than our love walk, which is the way we express God's love to others. Notice that it's God's love we're expressing—that's why we're enabled to show it even when we aren't feeling entirely loving toward someone. And it's only when we know the love of God that we can share that same love with others; in the words of the apostle John, *"Everyone who loves has been born of God and knows God. Whoever does not love does not know God, because God is love"* (1 John 4:7–8).

In order for us to walk in real love, God must be operating in our lives, for *"God is love."* When the Holy Spirit lives in us, we take on the nature of God and are thereby empowered to walk in love. Love is one of the fruits of the Spirit listed in Galatians 5:22–23; unlike gifts that are given, fruit is *grown*. We have to actively cultivate the fruit of love in our lives. Love cannot be faked; we can't pretend that we are walking in love, but we must truly put on love by clothing ourselves with this most important fruit of the Spirit.

God's Word calls love *"the most excellent way"* (1 Corinthians 12:31) and says that without love, we are nothing, and we gain nothing. (See 1 Corinthians 13:1–3.) The Father heart of God is filled with love for us, and His love is perfect. But what is love, exactly? And what is it not? Many of us grew up thinking of love as just one of the many emotions we experience. But we find a much richer definition in the Bible:

> *Love endures long and is patient and kind; love never is envious nor boils over with jealousy, is not boastful or vainglorious, does not display itself haughtily. It is not conceited (arrogant and inflated with pride); it is not*

rude (unmannerly) and does not act unbecomingly. Love (God's love in us) does not insist on its own rights or its own way, for it is not self-seeking; it is not touchy or fretful or resentful; it takes no account of the evil done to it [it pays no attention to a suffered wrong]. It does not rejoice at injustice and unrighteousness, but rejoices when right and truth prevail. Love bears up under anything and everything that comes, is ever ready to believe the best of every person, its hopes are fadeless under all circumstances, and it endures everything [without weakening]. Love never fails. (1 Corinthians 13:4–8 AMPC)

To evaluate our love walk, we can ask ourselves such questions as these: Do my thoughts, words, and actions line up with this biblical description of love? How about my heart attitude and my obedience? Comparing our attitudes, thoughts, words, and actions to this picture of love from God's Word gives us a clear reflection of who we really are. It lets us see whether we're being motivated by soulish desires or led by a spirit that's surrendered to God. That's because *"the word of God is alive and active. Sharper than any double-edged sword, it penetrates even to dividing soul and spirit, joints and marrow; it judges the thoughts and attitudes of the heart"* (Hebrews 4:12).

As we compare ourselves to the Word of God and yield to the leading of the Holy Spirit, we will find that loving others comes more naturally than it otherwise would. It is only by experiencing God's transformative love, and allowing that same love to channel through us, that we will fulfill God's command to love our enemies and pray for those who persecute us.

REFLECTION

1. Reread 1 Corinthians 13, either in this devotional or in your Bible, if you'd rather use a more familiar version. Then, jot down the aspects of love that you find the most challenging.

_____

_____

_____

2. Choose one of those challenging aspects of love and write it out below. Then, describe how Jesus perfectly fulfilled that aspect of love during His life on earth. (This would be a good opportunity to refresh your understanding of the biblical record of His life in the gospels: Matthew, Mark, Luke, and John.)

_____

_____

_____

3. Now, think about how you might embody that particular aspect of love...starting today. Write out some ideas and

then pray for God to help you to model biblical love, especially whatever aspect you've struggled with.

_____

_____

_____

Declaration

God is love, and since I'm walking with Him, He shows Himself through me.

PAVE THE WAY TO PEACE

There is no fear in love. But perfect love drives out fear, because fear has to do with punishment. The one who fears is not made perfect in love.
—1 John 4:18

If we are going to walk in true peace, we must be at peace with God, with ourselves, and with others. The peace that we experience is closely connected to our love walk. If we don't have peace, we'll find it extremely difficult to walk in love. And we can't live at peace with God until we have surrendered our hearts and lives to Him and to the leading of His Holy Spirit. Again, unless we have peace with God, we won't experience peace with ourselves or with others.

Peace with God is a prize without price. When we are at peace with God through a right relationship with Him, we can know His unconditional love for us. The acceptance of His love for us, and the acceptance of His wonderful works, enables us to live at peace with ourselves and, consequently, with who we are, how we look, how we feel about ourselves, and all other aspects of our lives. It is then, and only then, that we can live at peace with others.

The truth is that Jesus is the only source of true peace. And His peace is not the same thing that the world considers peace to be. Here's what He told His followers along these lines:

> *Peace I leave with you; My [own] peace I now give and bequeath to you. Not as the world gives do I give to you. Do not let your hearts be troubled, neither let them be afraid. [Stop allowing yourselves to be agitated and disturbed; and do not permit yourselves to be fearful and intimidated and cowardly and unsettled.]*
>
> (John 14:27 AMPC)

It's our choice whether we allow ourselves to get agitated or disturbed with ourselves and others. When we choose, instead, to receive and walk in the peace and love that our heavenly Father offers us, we can stop allowing painful, unsettling things to rule our lives. His peace comes as a result of our accepting Christ's love for us and then expressing it to others.

If we aren't walking in the love and peace of God, we become prey to the spirit of fear. Imperfect, unhealthy love produces fear; so do codependent and emotionally dependent relationships. But *"perfect love drives out fear"* (1 John 4:18), and *"God has not given us a spirit of fear, but of power and of **love** and of **a sound mind**"* (2 Timothy 1:7 NKJV). Fear is definitely a spirit. If God hasn't given us the spirit of fear, where do you think it came from? It came straight from the pit of hell. Satan delights when God's children are bound by any and every kind of fear: the fear of failure, the fear of man, the fear of abandonment, the fear of rejection, and so forth. We need to allow the Holy Spirit to reveal and uproot any fear from our lives so that we might walk in the love and peace of God.

Father wants us to be free to love and to be loved. Jesus summarized the whole of the law when He said, *"Love the Lord your God with all your heart and with all your soul and with all your mind* [and] *Love your neighbor as yourself"* (Matthew 22:37, 39). Love is the key to freedom and peace. Unless we love God wholeheartedly, we can't love our neighbors—or ourselves—and walk in peace with them, as God intends us to. Let the love of God drive out fear as you boldly show His love to others.

REFLECTION

1. Is there a human relationship in which you've been experiencing strain? If so, identify it here and consider jotting down a few details of your experience.

_____

_____

_____

2. Can you identify the root of fear that may have produced the strain in this relationship? Perhaps a fear of rejection? A fear of failure? A fear of loss?

_____

_____

_____

3. Pray about this relationship and turn it over to God, asking Him to replace fear with His peace and to bring lasting reconciliation and love.

_____

_____

_____

Declaration

*There is no room for fear but only peace
in my relationships.*

STEP INTO YOUR "POTENTIAL ZONE"

*We know that in all things God works for the
good of those who love him, who have been
called according to his purpose.*
—Romans 8:28

Just because we're called to have peace in our relationships does not mean that we are supposed to experience a *sense of peace* and comfort at all times. Otherwise, how would God spur us on to do bigger and better things for His kingdom? I've found that the key to stepping into our true potential—what I like to call the *potential zone*—is getting out of our comfort zone. And, believe me, this process is rarely easy! It requires that we lean on and trust the One who calls us in the first place.

One weekend shortly after I accepted Christ, our church's pastor announced an upcoming revival by a traveling evangelist. Over the course of attending the series of services, I felt that God wanted me to do what this man did—travel as an evangelist, telling people about God and preaching His Word.

It took me a while to digest the idea, and the enemy lied to me for a couple of years before I really stepped into my calling. I was a straight-A student in high school, but there was one class I did not enjoy in the slightest: oral communication. The thought of talking in front of a group of people completely overwhelmed me. On days when we had to deliver an oral presentation, I would sit there shaking, wringing my hands, and wiping my sweaty palms on my pants, while I anxiously thought to myself, *I'll go first to get it over with. No, I'll wait, in hopes that I'll be last.* I would get myself in a big tizzy over it!

When the Lord started speaking to me about working for Him, I began to rationalize why I couldn't do certain things. I told myself that I would marry a minister and thereby fulfill the call I felt to the ministry. My mind was plagued with so many lies the enemy had told me over the years that I was *boxed in* to seeing only my limitations. In a last-ditch effort to convince the Lord that I could never preach, I said, "But, Lord, I'm a woman!" He immediately responded, "Don't you think I know that? I'm the One who made you."

In my hunger for the things of God and my love for Him, I began taking small steps to follow His will for my life. I became a youth minister in my home church, with about five young people in my youth group. I thought, *Okay, five people—I can handle that.* I would study the Word and teach the young people on the weekends, but I made sure to stay in my comfort zone.

It wasn't long before I realized that if I was serious about coming into the full potential of what God had for me, I needed to kiss my comfort zone good-bye. No one comes into their potential zone unless they first get out of their comfort zone—a lesson that comes across especially strong in the Old Testament story of Abraham. In Genesis 12:1, the Lord told Abraham, *"Go from your country, your people and your father's household to the land I will show you."* Talk about getting way out of one's comfort zone! God required Abraham to not only leave the place that was familiar to him—a place that gave him a sense of security—but also the people to whom he had been emotionally attached. In order to obey God, Abraham had to travel to a land that was completely unknown to him—and he wasn't even certain where he was going.

Then, after God challenged Abraham to leave his comfort zone, He gave him a glimpse of his potential zone. He said, *"I will make you into a great nation and I will bless you; I will make your name great, and you will be a blessing"* (Genesis 12:2). In other words, God was saying, "This is your potential zone. Will you kiss your comfort zone good-bye in order to embrace your potential zone?" Later, perhaps in the most major discomfort-causing experience of all, Abraham was instructed by God to sacrifice Isaac, his only son, whom God had promised him and for whom Abraham had waited so long. (See Genesis 18:10; 21:1; 22:2.) It must have been an excruciating decision to obey God, but Abraham was faithful in stepping out of his comfort zone to follow the Lord. Speaking through one of His angels, God stopped Abraham from sacrificing his son, telling him, "*Now I know that you fear God, because you have not withheld from me your son, your only son*" (Genesis 22:12). The angel went on to deliver this wonderful message of promised blessing:

> *I swear by myself, declares the* LORD, *that because you have done this and have not withheld your son, your only son, I will surely bless you and make your descendants as numerous as the stars in the sky and as the sand on the seashore. Your descendants will take possession of the cities of their enemies, and through your offspring all nations on earth will be blessed, because you have obeyed me.*   (Genesis 22:16–18)

The choice to leave our comfort zones is always ours to make, and it's always at least a little unnerving. But whenever we choose to leave our comfort zone as an act of obedience to God, we can take comfort in the joy of obedience. And, later, we can reflect on all the blessings that came into our lives on the other side of our obedience, outside our comfort zone.

After I had served faithfully for several years as the youth minister at my church, the Lord began to open new doors for me. In my junior year of college, I transferred to a different school and became active in various campus ministries. My Father's hand of favor was forever extended to me as He wonderfully provided for my every need. It was during those final two years of undergraduate studies that God gave me a clear vision concerning my call to ministry. Again, I've rarely been in my comfort zone, but there's no place I'd rather be than in my potential zone with God.

REFLECTION

1. Think about your *comfort zone*, or the place where you feel at ease. Can you describe it? What are its most distinguishing features? How do you know when you're in that zone?

_____

_____

_____

2. Now, describe a time when you were called out of your comfort zone. How did that place end up being your potential zone?

_____

_____

_____

3. Has God ever asked you to do such difficult, uncomfortable things as He required of Abraham? What do you think was His aim?

_____

_____

_____

Declaration

I will go whenever God wants to get me out of my comfort zone and into my potential zone.

AVOIDING DETOURS AND DISTRACTIONS

*We fix our eyes not on what is seen, but on what is
unseen, since what is seen is temporary, but what is
unseen is eternal.*
—2 Corinthians 4:18

Many people attempt to reach their potential zone but never do because they get sidetracked by distractions that sometimes keep them from taking the first step of leaving their comfort zones. Others may take that first step, only to get lost due to a detour along the way. Some distractions are momentary diversions that quickly blossom into full-blown detours.

Over the years, my heart has broken time and again to see the Lord's servants lose everything as a result of detours. Many church leaders have used their gifts and talents for the kingdom of God, only to fall for detours designed by the enemy to destroy them, their families, their ministries, and the congregations that the Lord entrusted to their care. None of us is above falling into sin and compromise, so we must be aware of the enemy's schemes. We need to follow this exhortation of the apostle Peter:

> *Be alert and of a sober mind. Your enemy the devil prowls around like a roaring lion looking for someone to devour. Resist him, standing firm in the faith, because you know that the family of believers throughout the world is undergoing the same kind of sufferings.*

> (1 Peter 5:8–9)

We should avoid flirting with detours and instead seek to follow the leading of the Holy Spirit. *Flirting with detours* might consist in entertaining or meditating on thoughts that are opposed to what God has said. In many cases, we ask other people for their opinions on matters instead of going to God first in prayer. Even when we know what we should do because God has already told us, we try to talk ourselves—and let others talk us—into doing something different. We search for a second opinion—the one we really want to hear. Opinions from family members and friends are just one type of detour that may reroute us back to our comfort zones.

Flirting with detours can have devastating results. Because of detours, many people never reach their potential zone. Maybe you've taken a *pit stop* and allowed it to detour you. No matter how long you've been following a detour, the good news is, all you have to do is repent and ask the Lord to forgive you. When we confess our sins to God and repent of them, God *"is faithful and just and will forgive us our sins and purify us from all unrighteousness"* (1 John 1:9). He will also lovingly lead us out of our detour and place us back on the highway headed straight for the fulfillment of His wonderful purposes and plans for our lives.

Sometimes, relationships are the distraction that keeps someone from entering his or her potential zone. It was only after Abraham separated himself from his nephew Lot that he began to see his potential zone more clearly. (See Genesis 13:5–12.) Not everyone around us can see—or even wants to see—our potential zone. And there are times when the people around us block our own view of our potential zone. Just as Abraham had to separate himself from Lot before he could see all that God had for him, you may have to separate yourself from certain people—especially those who represent sin and invite compromise—in order to embrace your potential zone. I can tell you from firsthand experience, you will be glad you did. Moreover, others will be blessed by your stand for righteousness.

Another common distraction is that of intimidation. When Nehemiah determined to rebuild the wall around Jerusalem, he faced great opposition from the enemy. (See Nehemiah 4–6.) Yet he still chose to pursue his potential zone. When the enemy came to intimidate him, Nehemiah remained focused. He set out to rebuild the wall, and he did it!

As we pursue our potential zones, the enemy will recruit people, situations, and circumstances to mess with our plans and try to send us scurrying back to our comfort zones. He did it with Nehemiah, and He will do it with us. We need only to respond the way that Nehemiah did.

> *Sanballat and Geshem sent me this message: "Come, let us meet together in one of the villages on the plain of Ono." But they were scheming to harm me; so I sent messengers to them with this reply: "I am carrying on a great project and cannot go down. Why should the work stop while I leave it and go down to you?"*
>
> (Nehemiah 6:2–3)

Every time the enemy tries to send you a message of distraction, give him the *same* answer: "I don't have time for you. I'm pursuing my potential zone!"

REFLECTION

1. What are the main sources of distraction that seem to keep you trapped in your comfort zone or unable to reach your potential zone? Check all that apply.

_____ Relationships

_____ Social media

_____ Money/finances

_____ Career

_____ Idle pastimes

_____ Intimidation

___ Comparison

___ Other: _____

2. Release these distractions to God in prayer, and surrender daily to His power to overcome them.

3. Why do you think God wants you to make it to your potential zone? Can you see the impact your success would have on His kingdom?

_____

_____

Declaration

No detours or distractions will keep me from fulfilling God's plans for me.

IDENTIFY THE LIE

The thief comes only to steal and kill and destroy; I have
come that they may have life, and have it to the full.
—John 10:10

Another major source of distraction is discouragement. The devil loves to use negativity to douse our hopes and kill our dreams. There have been times in my life when I suddenly experienced an overwhelming feeling of discouragement, fear, or anxiety. Whenever this happened, I would stop and ask myself, *Why am I feeling this way? I was having a great day.* Over the years, the Holy Spirit showed me that these bouts of negativity usually result from a lie I had believed, whether consciously or unconsciously.

One of the enemy's most effective schemes against us is deception. Jesus described the devil's nature in this way: *"He was a murderer from the beginning, not holding to the truth, for there is no truth in him. When he lies, he speaks his native language, for he is a liar and the father of lies"* (John 8:44). The enemy spoke his native language to me for many years, and, for a while, I believed his lies. These lies were intended to stop me in my tracks, to paralyze me with the devastating emotional pain of his deception. And they worked.

But then—praise the Lord—God began to identify the lies that had been controlling my life: the lie that no one loved me, the lie that I was ugly, the lie that no one cared about me, and the lie that I was worthy of rejection. The more I studied God's Word, the more of His truth I absorbed. And the more of His truth I absorbed, the freer I became. Just as Jesus said in John 8:32, *"You will know the truth, and the truth will set you free."* The key word in this Scripture is *know*—it's the truth we know that sets us free. Truth can't set us free unless we know it, and not just as head knowledge but with our hearts and in our spirits. This type of knowing is a process that the Holy Spirit performs in our lives. As we allow the Lord to identify the devil's lies, the Holy Spirit can uproot the deception that might otherwise have grown into a stronghold.

Maybe you are boxed in today as a result of believing a lie of the enemy. Here are some lies to watch out for: *No one loves me. No one cares about me. I am rejected, and I'll never be accepted. I don't have what it takes to succeed. I don't have enough education. I wasn't born into the right family.* Now, that's a list of lies! When you begin to renew your mind by the truth and combat the lies, you allow God to rip open the box the enemy's put you in.

It's the enemy's lies that put us in the box, but it's God's truth in His Word that sets us free from that box. When we allow God to uproot the lies by the power of His Holy Spirit, all of the fears attached to the lies must go as well. Lies open the door for fears, but when you identify the lies and no longer accept them as truth, the fears attached to the lies will no longer have power in your life.

With the help of the Holy Spirit, I learned to identify the lie that was operating in every moment of negativity and thereby managed to trace the duplicitous thought back to something simple, such as something someone had said, a thought I had entertained about a situation, or some unexpected news I had received. As we seek the root of the lie, we can speak God's Word to the situation or circumstance and immediately take authority over it.

Again, God's Word tells us to take every thought captive and make it obedient to Christ. (See 2 Corinthians 10:5.) The thoughts we have about ourselves, the thoughts we have about others, and the thoughts we have about situations and circumstances must line up with God's Word if they are going to produce good fruit in our lives.

I want to encourage you today—don't buy the lie! Maybe the devil has tried to sell you a bunch of lies over the course of your life. Maybe there are falsehoods that you have believed for many years. Maybe there are little lies that the enemy throws at you every now and then in his attempts to discourage and distract you. Make a decision today to allow the Holy Spirit to uproot those lies so that you might live a victorious life in Jesus!

REFLECTION

1. The lies of the enemy are designed to distract and disable us in our pursuit of God's call on our lives. What has today's meditation taught you about how to identify the devil's lies? List some ways you can do this.

_____

_____

2. How have the lies that the enemy has spoken to you personally disabled you?

_____

_____

3. What are some of the lies the devil has spoken to you about yourself or a particular situation? Write them down, then go to God in prayer about them and wait on Him to give you His truth.

_____

_____

Declaration

*I will ignore the devil's lies and stand on the truth
of God's Word.*

Day 14

HOLD FAST TO THE TRUTH

If you hold to my teaching, you are really my disciples.
Then you will know the truth, and the truth
will set you free.
—John 8:31–32

When individuals who work with money are being trained to identify counterfeit currency, they study the real thing. They don't study the counterfeit; they study what a real twenty-dollar bill and a real hundred-dollar bill look like. If they are schooled in what a true bill looks like, they can spot a counterfeit quickly and easily. The same is true for us as God's children. When we study the real truth—the Word of God—we are able to identify Satan's counterfeits a mile away and can contradict them with the truth of God's Word. That's one reason it's so important to study the Word of God—so we will know the truth when we are confronted with a counterfeit argument from the enemy.

We see a prime example of this tactic at work in the biblical story of King Jehoshaphat. He received some alarming news, yet he didn't obsess over it. After he and the people of

Judah had inquired of the Lord through fasting and prayer, the word of the Lord came forth. God's response, as delivered by a man named Jahaziel, is recorded in the book of 2 Chronicles:

> *Listen, King Jehoshaphat and all who live in Judah and Jerusalem! This is what the LORD says to you: "Do not be afraid or discouraged because of this vast army. For the battle is not yours, but God's."* (2 Chronicles 20:15)

Jehoshaphat didn't buy the lie that the army of Judah would be destroyed by the vast army that was marching against them. And just like this biblical king, when we are confronted by a lie, especially when it's easy to believe, we need a word from the Lord. His Word is truth, and we need to be preoccupied with His Word alone about every situation.

Not only was the army of Judah victorious, but God fought the battle for them!

> *After consulting the people, Jehoshaphat appointed men to sing to the LORD and to praise him for the splendor of his holiness as they went out at the head of the army, saying: "Give thanks to the LORD, for his love endures forever."* (2 Chronicles 20:21)

Like Jehoshaphat's appointed men, we should rejoice in the truth after we've identified the lie. As the appointed men praised and worshiped God, they focused on God's report of the situation. We need to let the evil deeds of darkness, the lies of the enemy, be exposed by the light that is God's Word.

And as we do, we will be set free from the bondage of Satan, however long he's trapped us there.

For years, I was trapped by the fear of public speaking. I felt called by God to minister to people and to evangelize, yet I didn't think I was supposed to become a preacher. On top of that, I worried about how I would cover the expenses of my undergraduate studies, let alone seminary training. But because I felt sure of God's call on my life, I kept following Him, one step of faith at a time, and discovered time and again His faithfulness to provide for all my needs and to confirm my calling to preach. For a while, as I traveled with an evangelistic team from my university, I would hear certain words from the Lord that the young men on our team would preach on my behalf. God lovingly permitted me to remain in my comfort zone until I reached the place where I could face down the devil's intimidation and speak out for God by myself, filled with Holy-Spirit boldness.

Sure, I experienced moments of discomfort. At the first revival I led, for example, I got nervous and managed to deliver a forty-five-minute message in fifteen minutes. I spoke so fast that it probably sounded like I was speaking in tongues! But I kept on ignoring the devil's discouragement and submitting to God, one step of obedience at a time. And when I obeyed God and defied Satan's lies—lies that told me I couldn't preach, couldn't teach, and couldn't lead—I found favor and success.

Let's cling to the truth of God's Word and the special words of revelation He gives to us through His Holy Spirit, that we might ignore the lies of Satan and take a stand for the kingdom of God.

REFLECTION

1. If we know the truth, we can spot a lie without too much effort. Below are a few ideas of ways to keep the enemy from preoccupying our minds with lies. Select two or three to practice on a regular basis, that you might fill your mind with God's truth.

____ Bible study (personal)

____ Bible study (group)

____ Scripture memorization

____ Scripture-led prayer

____ Listening to hymns and other Christian music

____ Other: _____

2. Has there ever been a time when God gave you a special word or emphasized a certain truth in a way that enabled you to overcome some difficulty? Describe.

_____

_____

3. What have you been set free from because of knowing the truth?

_____

_____

Declaration

The truth of God trumps all the devil's tricks.

GUIDED BY THE TRUTH

*The steps of a [good] man are directed and established
by the Lord when He delights in his way
[and busies Himself with every step].*
Psalm 37:23 AMPC

Paying utmost attention to the truth—as outlined in God's Word and as revealed to us by special words from the Lord—has benefits that go beyond enabling us to contradict the devil's lies. God's Word is the ultimate road map of life, guiding us into proper attitudes that result in righteous living. So many people seem to be in a quandary when it comes to the will of God, wondering what He would have them do and what choice He would have them make in a particular situation. These people forget that God has revealed His will explicitly to us in the Bible.

When we align ourselves with God's will as revealed in His Word, we know that we're doing the right thing! As I like to say, hearing the voice of God is easy; it's walking in obedience to do what He's told us that's hard—hard on our flesh, that is. God requires our obedience, not our understanding.

We don't have to understand why God is telling us to do or not to do something; we have only to obey, trusting Him with the outcome.

The book of 2 Chronicles tells of a man named Hezekiah who prospered because of his obedience and hard work. *"In everything that he undertook in the service of God's temple and in obedience to the law and the commands, he sought his God and worked wholeheartedly. And so he prospered"* (2 Chronicles 31:21). It can be difficult to walk in obedience, but it's worth it because there are always blessings on the other side of our obedience. On the other hand, disobedience can tie the hand of God and hold back our blessings. (See, for example, Deuteronomy 28.)

Abraham received the promises of God because of his faith and obedience (see Hebrews 11:8–12, 17–19), and we can do the same today. As we step out in faith, doing what the Lord tells us to do—whether in His Word or as He prompts our spirits—we can walk in obedience and step into all that our heavenly Father has for us.

The problem sometimes becomes learning to let God set our course rather than mapping our own course and then looking to Him for affirmation. My first lesson in this truth came at the conclusion of my undergraduate studies. I was ready to go out and win the world for Jesus, so I planned to keep the university town as my home base while I traveled as a full-time evangelist. I felt a sense of security from having everything all mapped out. But, as I would learn, we shouldn't plot our own courses too specifically. *"In their hearts humans plan their course, but the* L ORD *establishes their steps"* (Proverbs 16:9). We can spend months *planning*, only to have the Lord use His *Holy Ghost eraser* and clear our calendars in a single moment.

As graduation day approached, Father God made His directions very clear to me. Before long, I knew without a shadow of a doubt that my next step was to attend graduate school. This step would be a real leap of faith, but I think you'll find that life's most rewarding, fulfilling pursuits are rarely reached with a leisurely stroll.

REFLECTION

1. There are always blessings on the other side of our obedience. List some of the "obedience blessings" you have received, and describe the step of obedience that prompted them.

_____

_____

2. God requires our obedience, not our understanding. Why do you think this is so?

_____

_____

3. When seeking direction, whom or what do you consult first? Ascribe chronological numbers to the following categories to give yourself a sense of where you're getting guidance.

____ God's Word

____ A trusted friend or family member

____ A neighbor

____ Google/Internet search results

____ Self-help books

____ Pastor

____ Teacher/professor

____ Counselor, psychologist, or psychiatrist

____ God

Declaration

By obeying God, I receive measureless blessing.

Day 16

OBEDIENCE DEMANDS
ABSOLUTE TRUST

*You will keep him in perfect peace, whose mind is stayed
on You, because he trusts in You.*
—Isaiah 26:3 NKJV

Shortly after I stepped out in faith and applied to graduate school, someone from the admissions office called to conduct a telephone interview. During the course of our conversation, the admissions counselor asked to confirm something I'd indicated on my application: that my savings and checking accounts had a balance of zero and I had no reliable source of income, such as a paying job. I found myself feeling grateful that it was a phone interview, for if we had been speaking face-to-face, I would have been crawling under the carpet at this point. "Yes, uh…that's correct, sir," I answered, knowing he probably thought I was crazy for applying to school when I couldn't afford the tuition, let alone all the other related expenses, or even such bare necessities as housing and food.

"How do you plan on paying for graduate school?" he asked me.

I mustered all my strength and, through quivering lips, answered, "I'm not exactly sure, sir. I only know that the Lord is telling me I'm supposed to go."

I was extremely surprised to hear him reply, "Well, if God's telling you to come, you'd better come."

I continued to take steps of faith toward attending graduate school. After receiving my acceptance letter, I was met with another pleasant surprise—an academic scholarship for my first year that would be renewed automatically for the second year, as long as I maintained a 3.8 grade point average (GPA). God was doing it again—His hand of provision met me at every step of obedience as I trusted in Him.

As a graduate student, I worked a couple part-time jobs and also traveled as an evangelist. I would wait tables during the week, scrape together all my tip money on Friday evening, and fill my gas tank early Saturday morning before driving to the revival I was scheduled to preach at that weekend, wherever it was located. Over the years, I decided that one of the best means of training for ministry is working as a server in the food industry, for it demands that you give your customers your very best, no matter what you receive in return. When I served and did everything *as working for the Lord* (Colossians 3:23), He provided for me, even if His provision didn't necessarily come from a source I expected.

The Lord was faithful, and, in spite of my busy schedule, He enabled me to maintain a GPA of 3.8, which meant that my scholarship was renewed for a second year. I eventually quit my part-time jobs and traveled as an evangelist just about every weekend. God miraculously provided for me, so that I graduated debt free. I didn't have ten cents to my name, but I had learned to rely on God at a whole new level and to obey Him at all costs.

We cannot begin to imagine the blessings in store for us if we'll only trust God and obey His every direction. Again, we may not understand why He's asking us to take a particular step; to us, His guidance may seem like the least logical course of action—case in point, the directive for me to enroll in graduate school, in spite of a lack of income! But when our steps are ordered by the Lord, as Psalm 37:23 says they are, then it means the Lord has placed our steps in a certain order for a reason. It reminds me of the children's activity *connect the dots*. Every one of our steps is a dot on the page. When all we can see is a bunch of dots, it doesn't make any sense, but when the Holy Spirit begins to connect the dots, we see clearly the beautiful picture that the Lord is making. Until that picture comes into focus for us, we need only to obey the Lord by taking one step of obedience at a time, in faith.

REFLECTION

1. Has God ever directed you to do something that didn't make sense to you at the time? What was your response?

_____

_____

2. The area of finances is often the hardest part of our lives to surrender to God. Consider the following categories and rate them in the order in which you feel comfortable trusting God, with 6 being the least and 1 being the most.

____ Finances

____ Health

____ Relations and friends (children, spouse, etc.)

____ Career

____ Material possessions

____ Education

3. Think about the areas you designated with the numbers 5 and 6, and pray that God would help you to increase your trust in Him in those areas, that you might surrender to His will, follow in complete obedience, and reap the resulting blessings.

Declaration

I have perfect peace in all circumstances because I trust in Jesus and commit to obey Him.

Day 17

GET UP OUT OF YOUR MESS

*Arise [from the depression and prostration in which
circumstances have kept you—rise to a new life]! Shine
(be radiant with the glory of the Lord), for your light has
come, and the glory of the Lord has risen upon you!*
—Isaiah 60:1 AMPC

I had learned to trust God when faced with the challenges—
financial and otherwise—of graduate school and then, not
long after, starting a career in the ministry. But I never could
have anticipated the hardships ahead. It wasn't long before I
married the man of my dreams and found myself pregnant,
only to find myself, three months later, relieved of my job
(along with health insurance), and then to reach the devastating realization that my husband was not who I thought he
was. I became a mother—and a *single* mother—in virtually
the same night. Being a single mom is the hardest thing I have
ever done. Yet I can say with complete honesty that it was in
my singleness, caring for a newborn on my own and facing
financial pressures as never before, that I came to know God
more intimately than ever before. And it was during this time

that I heard God say to me, "Get up out of your mess and go do what I've called you to do."

The first step in getting out of my mess was putting away the tissues. I spent the first nine or so months of my daughter's life crying tears of self-pity; each day was a struggle to survive. But when God told me to get out of my mess, He reminded me about what happened when Moses died. The law of Moses gave the Israelites thirty days to mourn the loss of their leader (see Deuteronomy 34:8); after that, Joshua was commanded by the Lord to arise and step into his new position as Moses's successor. (See Joshua 1:1–2.) Joshua had to release the old in order to embrace the new. In the same way, it is often when facing sorrows and disappointments that we're called to release the old so that we might step forward and embrace all the blessings Father God has for our future.

Joshua had to learn how to shoulder his new leadership responsibilities, and it's likely he didn't feel ready to do so. Just like Joshua, finding myself as a single mom, I faced a mountain of responsibilities I didn't much feel like handling, the least of which was finding a way to pay the bills now that my husband was out of the picture. I had to make a daily decision to release the old and embrace the new. As the Lord gently prompted me to release the *old*—the depression and desperation of my circumstances—I had to choose to embrace the *new*, life as a single mom. Father God continually reminded me that His plans for me had not changed; in spite of the *pit* I was in, He expected me to *"arise…shine,"* and fulfill His call on my life.

My call hadn't changed because of my circumstances. God's love for me hadn't changed due to my divorce and resulting difficulties. And neither had the fact that, together, He and I are the majority. *You* and God are the majority, too, because God is greater than any fear or foe. Take heart! When God calls us to get up out of our mess, we can be confident that as we choose to surrender the old and embrace the new, we are answering His call and making space for Him to bless us beyond our wildest imaginings, all to His glory.

REFLECTION

1. What would you say has been your hardest experience, to date? Have you been able to glean, by God's grace, any lessons or growth from this experience? Describe.

_____

_____

2. Has God ever required you to release something *old* in order to embrace something *new*? Describe your experience and reflect on its significance, if you feel so led.

_____

_____

3. Is there something you're clinging to today that you think God might be asking you to surrender to Him, painful though that process may be? Devote prayerful consideration to this matter and record any new impressions or leadings of the Holy Spirit.

Declaration

If God has called me to get up out of my mess,
I believe He will make a way for me to do so.

Day 18

SEED YOUR OWN NEED

*Let us not become weary in doing good, for at the proper
time we will reap a harvest if we do not give up.*
—Galatians 6:9

The early weeks and months of being divorced challenged me like nothing else had. During that time, I developed a new saying: "Life is hard, but God is good." I quickly learned that the harder life became, the more of God's grace and mercy I experienced. While it's true that I had never felt more helpless in my circumstances, the presence, love, and goodness of God were lavished on me like never before.

One day, I sensed the Lord telling me, "Seed your need and know where to sow." He was illuminating the biblical principle of reaping and sowing—"*A man reaps what he sows*" (Galatians 6:7)—that would enable me to persevere through my struggles. The meaning of Galatians 6:7 is that every seed produces according to its own kind. For example, tomato seeds produce tomatoes. Apple seeds produce apples. Orange seeds produce oranges. And in the same way, the seeds that we sow, whether for good or for evil, will produce predictable results.

When we sow encouragement into others, we reap encouragement ourselves. When we sow hope into others, we ourselves reap a harvest of hope. When we sow financial seed on solid, fertile soil, we reap financial blessings. Whatever we sow, that's what we'll reap. And the Lord used this principle to teach me to get my eyes off myself and the struggles I was going through. When He said to me, very clearly, "There's always someone hurting worse than you are. There's always someone who has been through more than you have," I realized I was supposed to sow my time, talent, and finances into the lives of individuals who were suffering more than I was. When I obeyed the Lord in this way, I experienced radical turnaround.

I started by actively seeking out women in great need. One night, between the hours of ten and eleven, the Lord prompted me to leave my house and go to the prayer room at church. Usually, I didn't go out that late in the evening, but the Lord was ordering my steps. I bundled my daughter into her baby carrier and drove to the church. There were other people present when I began to pray, and it wasn't long before I noticed another woman across the room who was sobbing uncontrollably. I went over to her and began to minister to her. I learned that she was in an abusive marriage and had just been beaten by her husband. I was blessed by the opportunity to sow encouragement, hope, and love into her life.

This became a regular thing for me; the Lord would direct me to women into whose lives I would sow, simultaneously seeding my own need. As I encouraged these women, *I* became encouraged. As I shared hope with them, *I* found myself filled with hope. It was an amazing confirmation of something God had told me in my early days of preaching: "Keep your eyes on Me and your heart on the needs of My people." Since the day He'd first said that, nothing had changed except my circumstances. I couldn't afford to let my circumstances get my focus stuck on *self* but instead needed to focus on serving others.

As time passed, the Lord continued to heal my heart as He ministered through me to many different women. One day, the Lord revealed to me that there were single moms living just a few miles from the church who didn't know how they were going to feed their children dinner that night. I didn't know how I was going to feed my daughter either. There's nothing like firsthand experience to help us develop a heart of compassion for those in need. The difference was, I *did* know who my Provider was. Isaiah 54:5 says, *"For your Maker is your husband—the Lord Almighty is his name."* My heavenly Husband had shown Himself to be flawlessly faithful to me, and I believed He would do the same for these other single moms to whom He had alerted me.

I began emptying my own pantry to fill grocery bags I then delivered to the single moms who lived in a subsidized housing development a few miles away. I would tell these women about the love of Jesus and how He died on the cross for the forgiveness of their sins. And every time I did this, I would return home to find a bag of groceries on my porch, courtesy of someone who had received a prompting from the Lord to bless me.

When we seed our own need, we reap an awesome harvest for ourselves, as well as for the kingdom of God!

REFLECTION

1. What is your usual response when you find yourself in need? Think of the last time you needed help with something—perhaps money, resources, advice, healing, or something else. Describe how you handled the situation and sought out help. What was the outcome?

_____

_____

2. Have you ever made a significant sacrifice in order to bless someone else, or do you typically act in a way that preserves the resources you have? Read the story of the widow's offering (Mark 12:41–44; Luke 21:1–4) and see if it doesn't change your attitude toward giving to others.

3. If you find yourself in need today, whether financially or otherwise, it may be that God is calling you to *seed your own need*. Can you think of someone you could reach out to and bless? What might you be able to do for that person to show them the love and grace of Jesus?

_____

_____

4. Supplemental reflection for those who need a better appreciation of God as their Husband:

Look up the following verses and summarize their implications to you as a bride of Christ Himself.

+ Philippians 4:19:

_____

+ Psalm 139:13–16:

_____

+ Psalm 34:7:

_____

Declaration

The Lord Almighty is my Husband and Provider;
He can provide for all of my needs!

TRANSFORM THROUGH THE STORM

Forget the former things; do not dwell on the past. See, I am doing a new thing…making a way in the wilderness and streams in the wasteland.
—Isaiah 43:18–19

I've said already that the hardest experience of my life—becoming a single mom—became the conduit to my closest intimacy with God. I was basically required to depend on Him for everything, and the resulting closeness has been an indescribable blessing. It's often true that we are transformed the most dramatically by the storms we go through, by life's most painful transitions. God's power will be made perfect in our weakness (see 2 Corinthians 12:9) if we just stand back and trust Him to work out His plan for us—a plan not for harm but for prosperity, hope, and a future, as He says in Jeremiah 29:11.

We are always transformed during times of transition; the outcome depends on whether we're trusting God all the way. When Father God transitions us from the old to the new, the process often brings us pain—whether physical, mental, emotional, or spiritual. But on the other side of these divinely ordained transitions is a total transformation that we wouldn't trade for anything. After every storm, we emerge transformed if we hang in there and persevere through the process, trusting God to carry us. A caterpillar changes from a creeping larva into a beautiful butterfly because it experiences a complete transformation within the chrysalis, and this transformation takes time. If the chrysalis is opened before that time has passed, the creature will die without ever becoming the lovely winged insect it was meant to be.

One way we can persevere patiently through times of transition is to *seed our need* and seek out others who are also in the midst of transitions. Our anointing can be the same as that of Christ Jesus according to this summary by the prophet Isaiah:

> *The Spirit of the Lord God is upon me, because the Lord has anointed and qualified me to preach the Gospel of good tidings to the meek, the poor, and afflicted; He has sent me to bind up and heal the brokenhearted, to proclaim liberty to the [physical and spiritual] captives and the opening of the prison and of the eyes to those who are bound.* (Isaiah 61:1 AMPC)

As God's children, we are anointed and qualified to minister the gospel to others. We can help our Christian brothers and sisters, as well as those who don't yet know Christ, through their times of transition, sharing the gospel, and offering our own testimonies as encouragement. In doing this, we ourselves will gain encouragement and gumption for our own times of transition—these storms that transform when God is at the helm of our tempest-tossed ship.

REFLECTION

1. Are you currently in a time of transition? If so, what do you perceive your destination to be? Are you letting God take control of your transformation process? Write out your thoughts, as well as a prayer, if you feel so led, in which you cede control to God and ask Him to take charge.

_____

_____

2. Think of a time when you were experiencing a painful transition and someone reached out with help or encouragement that really impacted you. What was it about this gesture that you found so significant? Prayerfully reflect on this and then record your thoughts.

_____

_____

3. Is there someone you know who is dealing with a particularly difficult transition? Prayerfully think about and then jot down some ways in which you might bless him or her such as praying, delivering a meal, or meeting over coffee for conversation. Then set a deadline for when you will carry out those goals.

_____

_____

Declaration

The One who formed me will transform me
according to His perfect plan.

DON'T NURSE IT, DON'T REHEARSE IT; JUST CURSE IT

Whatever is true, whatever is noble, whatever is right, whatever is pure, whatever is lovely, whatever is admirable—if anything is excellent or praiseworthy— think about such things
—Philippians 4:8

In the midst of any storm, one question we shouldn't be tempted to ask is the question "Why me? Why is this happening to me?" God will reveal the *why* to us in His perfect timing. Searching for the answer to that question in the midst of our storm is as unwise as searching outside for a favorite pair of shoes in the midst of a Category 5 hurricane. Wallowing in self-pity won't get us anywhere. Lamenting how *unfair* life has treated us will only produce heartache and will hinder our ability to be transformed in a fruitful way. As you can see, our attitude has a profound impact on the way we weather the storms of life.

One key to persevering through our storms, as revealed to me by the Lord, is to keep our mouths shut and our hearts right. Jesus said, *"Out of the abundance of the heart the mouth speaks"* (Matthew 12:34 NKJV). And Proverbs 4:23 instructs us, *"Above all else, guard your heart, for everything you do flows from it."* Our heart attitudes are either the wellsprings of life, as God intends for them to be, or the wellsprings of death. For some clarification, consider Proverbs 18:21: *"The tongue has the power of life and death."* The power of life and death is in my tongue, and out of the abundance of my heart, my mouth will speak. If my heart isn't right—if I am harboring anger, bitterness, offense, and negativity—then my mouth will give voice to these negative heart attitudes, speaking words of death rather than life.

We need to guard the attitudes of our hearts and the words we speak when we're weathering our storms. One day, speaking of hurts, the Lord said to me, "Don't nurse it, don't rehearse it; just curse it in the name of Jesus." We can't afford to sit around *nursing* our hurts and wounds with such thoughts as these: *"No one else has things as rough as I do." "Life just isn't fair." "Nobody loves me, everybody hates me; I may as well go eat worms."* Eat worms? No, thank you. The Word of God says we will eat the fruit of our words: *"The tongue has the power of life and death, and those who love it will eat its fruit"* (Proverbs 18:21, the entire verse this time). If we choose to verbally rehearse all the *worms* in our lives, then we ought to be prepared to savor their flavor.

When we rehearse the emotional hurts in our lives, we describe every detail of our *worms* to anyone who will listen, repeating the same old things over and over. Twenty years down the road, we're still shoving our worms down other people's throats as we continue to verbally rehearse and rehash our hurts. But if we curse the hurts in the name of Jesus, we uproot the devastating effects of any stronghold that the enemy has been trying to plant in our lives. When we take every hurt, every disappointment, and every rejection to the foot of the cross of Jesus, we can walk freely in the forgiveness that we've offered to our offenders—the same forgiveness that Christ has extended to us. If we are going to succeed in getting up out of our messes, we must keep our mouths shut and our hearts right! Is that easy to do? No way. But is it worth it? Absolutely!

REFLECTION

1. Rewrite in your own words the phrase, "Don't nurse it, don't rehearse it; just curse it in the name of Jesus." Why is this practice so important?

_____

_____

2. Is there a hurt you've been rehearsing? Write it down and then write a declaration of the opposite effect, proclaiming your faith in Jesus to prompt a complete turnaround in your circumstances.

_____

_____

3. Are there any phrases you find yourself saying, or thoughts you find yourself thinking, that keep you trapped in a pit of negativity? Write them down and then cross them out. Then, pen a prayer of release, surrendering those thoughts to God and asking Him to replace them with His hope and promises of a future.

_____

_____

_____

_____

Declaration

I curse all doubts and negative thoughts, and declare them vanquished in the name of Jesus!

Day 21

ABIDE IN THE VINE

Dwell in Me, and I will dwell in you.
—John 15:4 AMPC

We can try our best to eliminate negative words from our vocabulary and despairing thoughts from our minds, but our self-effort will get us only so far. The truth is, it's impossible to maintain an attitude of godly perseverance and peace in the midst of our storms unless we're abiding in the Vine—dwelling continually in the presence of Jesus.

Here is now Jesus described the practice of abiding in the Vine:

> I am the True Vine, and My Father is the Vinedresser. Any branch in Me that does not bear fruit [that stops bearing] He cuts away (trims off, takes away); and He cleanses and repeatedly prunes every branch that continues to bear fruit, to make it bear more and richer and more excellent fruit. You are cleansed and pruned already, because of the word which I have given you [the teachings I have discussed with you]. Dwell in Me, and I will dwell in you. [Live in Me, and I will live in you.]

Just as no branch can bear fruit of itself without abiding
in (being vitally united to) the vine, neither can you bear
fruit unless you abide in Me. (John 15:1–4 AMPC)

We draw our strength and nourishment from the vine that
we are abiding in. When we abide in anything but the Lord, it
is detrimental to our survival. Only when we are abiding in the
True Vine can our lives bear the fruit of the Spirit—*"love, joy,*
peace, forbearance, kindness, goodness, faithfulness, gentleness and
self-control" (Galatians 5:22–23). Jesus is the True Vine, but
there are many false vines that we can end up abiding in, if we
aren't careful. We can remain in constant stress and turmoil,
burned out by trying to make it through the storm in our own
strength. We can bow to the pressures of the world and deal
with our storms in ungodly, futile ways. Or, we can remain in
the True Vine—we can stay in His presence, submit to His
Word, and come successfully through every storm, no matter
the source of the wind and rain.

If we abide in the Vine, then God, the *"Vinedresser,"* can
use our storms to prune us so that we become even more fruitful. What Satan means for evil, God will use for our good,
as He did for Joseph (see Genesis 50:20), if we just keep our
hearts right. Father God is the One who does the pruning,
so we can stop blaming those around us for this process that
can, admittedly, be pretty painful sometimes. Many people
don't want to submit to the pruning process, so they *become*
prunes—bitter, angry, spiritually dried-up people—instead of
letting God prune them into the spiritually strong, fruitful

individuals He intends for them to be. I want to challenge you not to become a prune but to submit to the pruning process. Allow the Lord to produce great fruit in you and through you, even in the midst of your storms.

When I put the past behind me and refused to wallow in self-pity because of my separation from my husband and my single-mom status, the Lord healed my broken heart and showed me that the best thing I could do for my daughter, other than bringing her up to know the Lord, was to be a healthy, emotionally whole mother who loved her. As a single parent, I have been able to teach her that the Lord truly is a Father to the fatherless; He's our faithful Provider and Protector.

What are you abiding in today? If you're not sure, check the fruit you're producing, *"For every tree is known by its own fruit"* (Luke 6:44 NKJV). The fruit you produce will indicate whether you're abiding in the True Vine or dwelling in the garden of self-determination. Come to the Vinedresser, for His pruning is gentle and His love is enough to see you through any storm.

REFLECTION

1. Where are you abiding? Evaluate your fruit. For every pair of terms, place a check beside the one you feel you exhibit more often.

___ Patience	___ Impatience
___ Forgiveness	___ Holding grudges
___ Pardoning	___ Placing blame
___ Speaking gently	___ Shouting angrily
___ Calm spirit	___ Turmoil
___ Contentment	___ Discontent
___ Joy	___ Despair
___ Integrity	___ Disloyalty

Which column had more checkmarks? Prayerfully mull over your results and write out any reflections here.

_____

_____

2. Do you know someone who abides in the Vine? Describe that person in detail, making sure to include examples of ways in which he or she demonstrates a commitment to the Lord.

_____

_____

3. Is God asking you to submit to His pruning process in a certain area of your life? Have you been resisting His invitation? If so, surrender to Him in prayer, asking Him to have His way with you. I promise, you won't regret it!

Declaration

I choose to abide in the Vine and produce great fruit for the kingdom of God.

DOUBT YOUR DOUBTS AND FACE YOUR FEARS

*Do not fear, for I am with you; do not be dismayed, for I
am your God. I will strengthen you and help you; I will
uphold you with my righteous right hand.*
—Isaiah 41:10

One day early on in my single parenting journey, the Lord revealed to me that I was filled with all kinds of fears. He said, "If you are going to fulfill the call I have on your life, you must doubt your doubts and face your fears."

It's true that I was filled with a lot of doubt. I doubted that I could continue in the ministry as a divorced single mother. I doubted that we could pay all our bills. But the Lord began to remind me that these doubts were merely whispers of the devil, who is *"a liar and the father of lies"* (John 8:44). Then God told me, "You need to doubt those doubts." So, whenever a doubt would enter my mind, I would simply say out loud, "I doubt that! I know God is going to provide. I doubt that! I know God's going to fulfill His call on my life." It worked. Faith began to grow in my heart, and the doubts slowly faded.

After doubting my doubts, I had to face my fears with faith. The first of my fears God dealt with was the fear that I wouldn't be provided for—a fear that was rooted in childhood, when the financial pressures my family faced weighed heavily on me. One day, during a time of prayer, God impressed upon me the fact that it was nothing for Him—the great, big God of the universe—to provide for the needs of myself and my daughter, which, in the grand scheme of things, were pretty minor.

The years following this revelation were exciting as I experienced time and again the miraculous provision of my heavenly Father. The most looming expense I faced was my monthly mortgage payment, and yet, every month, the Lord came through for me. I didn't always appreciate the way His provision came—always at the midnight hour—or that He often called me to humble myself and ask a certain person for the money I needed. Other times, I wasn't permitted to ask anyone for help. There was a woman at church who always asked me if there was anything I needed, and the only thing God permitted me to say to her was, "Yes, I need diapers for my daughter." All the while, I was thinking, *Lord, I need a lot more than diapers!* But I soon realized that God desired my obedience because He was patiently building faith in my heart.

REFLECTION

1. What are some doubts that have hounded you recently? Check all that apply.

____ I doubt that God loves me.

____ I doubt that God can forgive me.

____ I doubt that my needs will be met.

____ I doubt that God can turn my situation around and use it for good.

____ I doubt I will be fulfilled.

____ I doubt I will overcome a certain struggle.

___ I doubt _____.

2. Now it's time to doubt your doubts! Search the Scriptures (using an online resource, if it helps) to find verses that contradict these lies of Satan. Write them down and commit them to memory in order to encourage yourself the next time doubts come creeping in.

_____

_____

3. Go to God in prayer about your doubts and fears, and make sure to listen for His still, small voice. One word from the Lord is enough to defeat all manner of doubt, so give Him

space to speak! Be sure to record any impressions He gives you or Scriptures He brings to mind.

_____

_____

Declaration

My doubts and fears can't stand in the presence of Jesus!

Day 23

GOD, YOU'VE GOT MAIL!

Cast all your anxiety on [God] because he cares for you.
—1 Peter 5:7

In the midst of financial hardship, it can be tempting to become bitter and resentful toward those around us whom we *think* should be helping us out. But we should always look to the Lord for our provision rather than expect or demand that other people supply our needs. Even though I learned this lesson long before becoming a single mom, there was one day when I sat staring at my file cabinet, thinking of the bulging folder of bills marked "Due," and getting angrier by the second. I felt almost indignant that there were people in my life who could have written a single check to cover all of my bills and wouldn't have even missed the amount. The Lord gently admonished me with the reminder that He was my heavenly Father and could easily cover my every expense.

I realized that God not only *could* pay my bills but that He *would*, if I would just trust Him—day by day. When Jesus taught His disciples to pray (see Matthew 6:9–13), He included the phrase *"Give us today our **daily** bread"* (verse 11).

He didn't say, "Give us today our monthly bread." I don't know about you, but I kind of like to have the whole month budgeted out—or, better yet, the whole year! But God doesn't usually work that way. He requires us to walk by faith and place our total trust in Him.

After the Lord reminded me that He could meet my needs, I began to treat every incoming bill as if it had His name on it instead of mine. Whenever I found a stack of bills in my post office box, I would simply look up and say, "God, You've got mail!" Then I would take those bills home and file them away until I earned or received money, at which point I would say, "Okay, God. Which of Your bills do You want me to pay for You now?"

The Lord taught me to take comfort in the knowledge that everything I have comes from Him. Every dollar, every pantry staple, every article of clothing—everything comes from Him. He also taught me to ask Him what He wanted me to do with every dollar that came into my hands. Looking to Him for stewardship guidance was an important key to having all my needs met.

Philippians 4:19 says, *"My God will meet all your needs according to the riches of his glory in Christ Jesus."* If my needs aren't met, then something is wrong. Maybe I spent God's money on something I wanted or thought I needed instead of paying one of His bills or giving to His church. As we learn to ask God what He wants us to do with every resource He puts in our hands, we can be free from stress and worry, and we can say, "God, You've got mail!"

REFLECTION

1. When you find yourself in need, where do you tend to look for help? Your family? Your friends? Your pastor? Your neighbors? Do you make your needs known or simply expect these people to intuit your state of need? In the space below, reflect on your attitude and behavior when in a place of need.

_____

_____

2. "God, You've got mail!" became, for me, an empowering declaration that automatically lightened my mood and boosted my faith. Is there a similar phrase you could say when facing pressing financial obligations, health concerns, relational conflicts, or other issues?

_____

_____

3. God wants us to trust Him day by day, moment by moment. Of course, it's prudent to plan ahead, but sometimes,

our advance planning can put us in panic mode. Try using that phrase, *"Give us today our daily bread"* (or *"Give me today my daily bread"*) when bringing your financial concerns to God in prayer, and see if it doesn't boost your faith and calm your fears.

Declaration

*My God shall supply all my needs according
to His glorious riches!*

Day 24

THE SPEED OF SUDDENLY

With God all things are possible.
—Matthew 19:26

When God shows up to meet our needs, He often shows up *suddenly*. On the day of Pentecost, "**suddenly** *a sound like the blowing of a violent wind came from heaven and filled the whole house where they were sitting*" (Acts 2:2). When Paul was persecuting the Christians, "**suddenly** *a light from heaven flashed around him*" (Acts 9:3), and he fell to the ground in a great encounter with God. When Peter was in prison, "**suddenly** *an angel of the Lord appeared*" (Acts 12:7) who caused his chains to come off and then led him to freedom.

Today, God still moves at the speed of *suddenly*. When God's will and God's timing intersect, you suddenly receive your breakthrough; the promise of God is suddenly fulfilled after you have waited patiently. Therefore, we must always expect our next *suddenly* from the Lord. If we aren't expecting it, we won't be ready when it comes. Our next *suddenly* is just up ahead, so we'd better get ready. We don't want to miss that business deal, ministry opportunity, or job opening we have been waiting for.

When God suddenly provides or acts on our behalf, He usually requires sudden action on our part—immediate, total obedience to the leading of the Holy Spirit. If God suddenly says, "Give," we'd better give suddenly. If God suddenly says, "Pray," we'd better pray suddenly. If God suddenly says, "Go there and do this," we'd better go there and do what He says. As we take care of the sudden actions that God is requiring of us, He will take care of His sudden actions on our behalf.

If the Lord prompts you to take a job that pays half the salary you are making now, you'd better obey. If the Lord tells you to move to a different city, but you'd rather stay where you are, you'd better move anyway. The key is obedience. As we submit to the will of the Father as expressed through the leading of the Holy Spirit, we will step into God's abundant provision. But if we resist the Father's leading and go our own way, we will never have enough because the Father's provision is always at His place of positioning.

Isaiah 1:19 says, *"If you are willing and obedient, you will eat the good things of the land."* The key word here is *"if."* It depends upon our choices. *If* we are willing and obedient, we will step into God's best for us. It's easy to be willing but harder to be obedient. Many times, I've prayed, "Lord, help me be willing to be obedient." Matthew 26:41 says, *"The spirit is willing, but the flesh is weak."* We have to carry out our willingness in the form of obedience. If our flesh submits to the Spirit, and we walk in obedience, we set ourselves up to receive God's blessings. Obedience always brings blessings.

Father knows the awesome plans He has for your life—*"plans to prosper you and not to harm you, plans to give you hope and a future"* (Jeremiah 29:11)—and He wants you to know His plans for you, as well. You can know when your *suddenly* is on the horizon if you maintain a life of prayer, which will enable you to hear God's voice and sense His direction. Then, when you are clued in on the plan, you can expect your *suddenly*—a *suddenly* filled with hope, prosperity, and a bright future.

Today, when I look back over my life, I can honestly say, "God is so good." Many of the storms that I have been through seem as though they were from another lifetime. *Suddenly* the sun was shining again. *Suddenly* a new day appeared on the horizon. *Suddenly* the pain dissipated from my heart. *Suddenly* the Son was shining through me with a new and glorious brightness. *Suddenly!*

REFLECTION

1. Can you recall a time when God showed up suddenly for you? If so, describe it.

_____

_____

2. When God suddenly acts on your behalf, He often requires sudden action on your part. What form of action

might He be demanding of you today? Pray that He would give you the strength and faith to respond in obedience.

3. Memorize Jeremiah 29:11, as it appears below, inserting your own name. Know that God is intimately familiar with every detail of your life and wants to do great things in and through you!

"For I know the plans I have for [   ]," declares the LORD, *"plans to prosper [   ] and not to harm [him/her], plans to give [   ] hope and a future."*

Declaration

Suddenly, God will show up for me!

PROVISION FROM UNLIKELY PLACES

*My God will meet all your needs according to the
riches of his glory in Christ Jesus.*
—Philippians 4:19

I was preparing for my second citywide evangelistic youth crusade, and I was starting to worry. My deposit to the convention center where the event would be held was due the next day, and I was still short by seven grand. After speaking at a Sunday morning church service, I felt the Lord telling me to drive to a city that wasn't on my speaking agenda, for a service where I was surprised to hear the youth pastor mention the very crusade for which I was preparing. Someone in the congregation made him aware that I was present, and the pastor asked me to come to the front and share a bit about the crusade. When I'd concluded my remarks, the pastor took the microphone and said to the congregation, "This is a God thing, and if God tells you to help her in any way, please do." At the close of the service, I was talking to various people and was separated from a friend who was traveling with me. When the crowd dispersed, I was standing alone with no financial gift. But when I met up with my friend, she showed me a check for $7,000 that a woman had written when she learned how much money we needed.

On another occasion, the Lord directed me to travel to Tampa, Florida, to visit some pastors I knew. *Go to Florida?* I thought in disbelief. *I've had to believe God for gas money just to get around town, and He's saying, 'Go to Florida'?* Nevertheless, acting on faith, I made travel plans as if I had all the money I needed in the bank. I arranged for a friend to travel with me to help with my daughter, then nine months old, but told no one of my financial need. As our departure day approached, I didn't have five cents. What I *did* have was a big file folder labeled "Due," filled with God's bills. The day before we left, I helped a friend with her yard sale, then went home to pack. I was loading the van when a woman from church showed up with two bags of diapers and thirty jars of baby food, saying, "God put it on my heart to bring these to you today." I praised God for His provision, sharing with my friend about our travel plans. As if that wasn't enough to rejoice over, there was another knock on my door at eleven o'clock that night. My friend who'd had the yard sale handed me a plastic baggie filled with money, saying God had told her to give all her proceeds to me. The amount equaled what I'd calculated we would need for gas. Praise God! Then, while I was in Florida, the Lord moved the hearts of several ministers to bless me financially, though they had no idea of my needs.

We can count on Father God to get His provision into our hands, but we usually can't predict the channel by which He will send it to us. Often, He uses the least expected or seemingly unlikeliest channel. I'm convinced that the Lord *sets us up* to *build us up*. The setup is that the necessary funds almost never come from the expected source, and the buildup is for our faith. The Father builds up our faith during every step of this marvelous journey we are on with Him.

REFLECTION

1. God often gets His provision into our hands using a channel we never expected. Why do you suppose He does this?

_____

_____

2. Have you ever received provision from an unlikely source? Describe what happened and how you felt.

_____

_____

3. Our verse for today is Philippians 4:19—definitely a Scripture worth committing to memory! First, use an online

Bible study tool to read Philippians 4:19 in as many different Bible translations as you can. Then memorize that verse in whatever Bible version(s) speak the most to you, and see how many times it comes to mind during the day. God's Word will not return to Him void! (See Isaiah 55:11.)

Declaration

*My God can and will supply anything
and everything I need.*

Day 26

ONE STEP OF OBEDIENCE
AT A TIME

*Teach me to do your will, for you are my God; may your
good Spirit lead me on level ground.*
—Psalm 143:10

Another part of the *great setup* of God's provision is that God will give us instructions that don't make sense to our natural minds; unless we follow these instructions, we won't receive our miraculous provision. As I was driving home from Tampa, the Lord spoke to me again and told me that it was time to start my television ministry. Joy Ministries had recently been offered local airtime, but I wasn't sure we were ready, especially in a financial sense. But God's timing is not our timing, just as His ways are not our ways. (See Isaiah 55:8.) When God does things, His ways and His timing are such that we couldn't try to take the credit, even if we wanted to. It was very obvious to me, and to everyone around me, that it was God who had opened the door for my television ministry to begin.

Several local ministries had offered to let me borrow their television equipment and even their church buildings to begin recording my television program, but none of those leads panned out. Just as I started to feel discouraged, the Lord said to me, "Just use what you have." I thought, *Okay, I have my house and I have my car.* God responded, "That's right—use your house." It definitely wasn't what I'd been planning, but because God spoke to me, I went ahead and started recording my television program in my own living room.

God was teaching me to listen to His voice. I had known for some time what God had called me to do, but I'd been wondering for months how I could possibly reach the point of answering that call. In the months following my road trip to Tampa, the Lord revealed to me a spiritual truth I will never forget: we get to where we are going one step of obedience at a time.

As I took small, daily steps of obedience according to what God was telling me to do, the call of God on my life continued to unfold, and His provision continued to flow. Because I listened to the leading of the Holy Spirit more than the leading of my bank account, many people were saved and encouraged by watching on TV as I preached under the anointing of the Holy Spirit in my tiny, unglamorous living room. With a blue bedsheet strung up behind me and a rented pulpit before me, I spoke because God told me to, and lives were changed.

My life has been marked by countless instances of God showing up to meet and even exceed my needs in miraculous ways. What He's done for me, He will do for you, too, if you'll take one step of obedience at a time and prioritize His leading over any other authority. Remember, His plans are to prosper you! (See Jeremiah 29:11.) Listen to Him and follow His lead. You won't regret it.

REFLECTION

1. Has God ever given you instructions that seemed illogical? If so, describe the instructions and your own response. What were the results?

_____

_____

2. Why do you think God gives us instructions that don't make any sense to our natural minds?

_____

_____

3. Following the leading of the Holy Spirit requires that we learn to hear His *"still small voice"* (1 Kings 19:12 NKJV). This ability takes practice. Commit to spending ten to twenty minutes a day reading God's Word and following up your Bible study with a time of silence, inviting the Holy Spirit

to illuminate Scripture and impress upon you anything He would have you know or do.

Declaration

I will listen to the Lord above everything else!

Day 27

TRUE SUCCESS

Blessed is the one who trusts in the LORD,
whose confidence is in him.
—Jeremiah 17:7

I was in my mid-twenties when I organized my first citywide crusades. I remember renting out a big convention center in downtown Oklahoma City and thinking that because I was following God in obedience, people would flock to the meeting by the thousands. When that didn't happen, I felt like a failure. The Lord asked me, "Did you do what I told you to do?" I said, "Yes, Lord."

"Then you were successful," He responded. "Success is doing what I told you to do."

The Lord went on to show me that if I took the responsibility on myself for having a small crowd, I would later take the glory for having a large crowd. The degree of my obedience was important, not the size of the crowd. (See Judges 7.)

Years later, when my husband and I divorced, I felt like a failure all over again. I had done everything I could think to do to save my marriage—I had stood in faith for the restoration of our relationship, and fasted and prayed for my husband's deliverance—without achieving my desired result. I had to press past my feelings of failure and remind myself that because I had walked in obedience to the Lord every step of the way, *I* was not a failure, even though my marriage had failed. In addition, I focused on a significant longing for a child that had been fulfilled through my marriage. Though hope deferred makes the heart sick, all the longings fulfilled in our lives are trees of life. (See Proverbs 13:12.)

The Father wants to raise up the winner in me, in you, and in all of us who call Jesus our Savior. If true, lasting success is our desire, then we need to remember where our victory lies— in dwelling in the presence of the Lord Almighty. *"He who dwells in the secret place of the Most High shall abide under the shadow of the Almighty"* (Psalm 91:1 NKJV). As we dwell in the secret place of the Most High through prayer, worship, Bible study, and surrender to His will, we can experience the Person and presence of the Holy Spirit—and that's the essence of winning!

The Holy Spirit is a Person who desires continual fellowship with us. He's the greatest Comforter, Counselor, and Helper we could ever hope for (see, for example, John 14:26); He leads and guides us into all truth. (See John 16:13.) He will reveal to us all kinds of things we never could have known without spending time listening to His voice, things that will equip us for true, lasting victory. That's why we need to quiet ourselves before the Lord, training ourselves to hear the gentle leading of His *"still small voice"* (1 Kings 19:12 NKJV.)

REFLECTION

1. What is true success, as seen from God's perspective?

_____

_____

2. We are winners when we surrender to the leading of the Holy Spirit. Look up the following Scriptures that talk about the Holy Spirit, and jot down a summary of each one, making sure to note any details that make a particular impression on you.

♦   Psalm 143:10

_____

_____

♦   John 14:26

_____

_____

+ John 16:13

_____

_____

+ 2 Corinthians 3:17

_____

_____

+ Romans 5:5

_____

_____

+ 1 Corinthians 3:16

_____

_____

3. Go to God in prayer, asking that He would reorient your definition of success and allow yourself to be led by His Holy Spirit. Feel free to write out your prayer and to pray it again as often as you feel like it!

_____

_____

Declaration

Victory is mine because I dwell in the presence of the Holy Spirit.

Day 28

WHINING VERSUS WINNING

Out of the abundance of the heart the mouth speaks.
—Matthew 12:34 NKJV

One sure way to miss the quiet messages of the Holy Spirit is to keep on whining, whether aloud or in our hearts. God's regular communication with us depends on how well we are able to quiet ourselves and listen to His Spirit. The enemy and our circumstances will present us with daily invitations to whine. We must decide to silence the whiner within, so we can become winners with God! Today, I want to give you a short list of the main differences between whiners and winners, so you can train yourself to be in the latter category.

First of all, whiners lack patience and hate to wait. Winners, on the other hand, understand that waiting is a big part of life, with waiting on the Lord being at the top of the list. *"Blessed are all who wait for him!"* (Isaiah 30:18). And Psalm 27:14 exhorts us to *"wait for the LORD; be strong and take heart and wait for the LORD."* Winners respect God's timing and are blessed as a result. They can say with the psalmist, *"I waited patiently for the* LORD; *he turned to me and heard my cry*" (Psalm 40:1).

Whiners never want to get out of their comfort zones; if they happen to step outside those bounds, you are sure to hear about it in the form of complaints and statements of self-pity. Winners, on other hand, pursue their potential zones, acknowledging the challenge but seeing the value. Even Jesus had to press past His comfort zone, in the most challenging act ever performed by a human. Just before He was arrested and then crucified, He prayed in desperation, *"My Father, if it is possible, may this cup be taken from me. Yet not as I will, but as you will"* (Matthew 26:39). He was saying, in other words, "What You are asking of me is way outside My comfort zone, but if that's what's required to bring me into My potential zone and to fulfill Your purposes for Me, then I yield to Your will!"

Whiners always ask, "What if?" and fear the worst; they want to play it safe. Winners ask, "Why not?" and go for it when God gives the signal. They don't make rash decisions; instead, their boldness comes from listening to God and then getting out of the boat to walk on water when He says it's time. (See, for example, Matthew 14:25–29.) Whiners fixate on their limitations, while winners see what *can* be, and trust God to make their possibilities into realities. They live by Philippians 4:13: *"I can do all this through him who gives me strength."* Whiners tend to harbor a victim mentality, whereas winners maintain a positive, faith-filled outlook that counts on victory through Jesus.

In short, whiners allow failure to become their identity and their destiny; winners recognize failure as an opportunity to learn and grow. They remember that as long as they're following God faithfully, success and victory are theirs. *Let's decline to whine* and adopt a winner's mentality, rejoicing in our ultimate victory through Christ Jesus!

REFLECTION

1. Summarize some key differences between whiners and winners.

_____

_____

2. Looking again at the list you just made, which characteristics do you identify with the most? In other words, would you generally classify yourself as a whiner or a winner?

_____

_____

3. Over the next hours and days, pay attention to your attitudes, thoughts, and spoken words, in regard to whether they reflect those of a whiner or a winner. Write down a

description of any of these that stand out to you, and then, for the instances of *whining*, envision how a winner would have responded. This written rehearsal will prime you to respond more like a winner the next time a similar circumstance arises.

_____

_____

Declaration
*I can stop whining and live like a winner
because Christ Jesus dwells within me!*

Day 29

THE BATTLE BELONGS TO
THE LORD

The battle is not yours, but God's.
—2 Chronicles 20:15

We've established that we are victors when the Lord God is on our side, for *"God…gives us the victory through our Lord Jesus Christ"* (1 Corinthians 15:57). Our heavenly Father doesn't want us wearing ourselves out trying to fight the battles we're facing, whether financial, spiritual, emotional, or another type, because every battle belongs to Him. (See 2 Chronicles 20:15.)

Even when we believe that God is fighting for us, so many of us struggle with surrendering our weapons and letting the Lord fight the enemy in our stead. The Israelites were no different. When Moses was leading God's people out of Egypt, only to have Pharaoh and his army chase them down, they were terrified; "Wouldn't it have been better to remain enslaved in Egypt and die there than be hunted down now?" they whined to Moses (see Exodus 14:12). They assumed that they would need to defend themselves—surely without success—against their aggressors. But I love how Moses responded:

> *Do not be afraid. Stand firm and you will see the deliverance the* LORD *will bring you today. The Egyptians you see today you will never see again. The* LORD *will fight for you; you need only to be still.* (Exodus 14:13–14)

The only thing we need to do if we're going to let God fight our battles is to master our fears, because fear always activates our efforts to control. If you fear having too little money, you will try to control your finances. If you fear rejection, you will work to seal yourself off from any relationship that might expose you to the pain of rejection. When you're fearful, you can't surrender to God and fully trust Him to see you through. Yet when you face your fears by the power of the Holy Spirit and then relinquish control to the Lord, you can operate in full faith.

Things have to be truly beyond our control in order for them to be in God's control. Sometimes, God has to use one of His divine *setups* to help us cede control to Him. I've had this very experience on many occasions, especially in regard to my finances. Early on in the ministry, I often wondered whether I should pursue a more lucrative career, since it was always tough making ends meet. One memorable day, I was nearing the due date of a mortgage payment and didn't know where the money would come from. I did everything I knew to do, talked to everyone I could think to ask—and still nothing. At the end of the day, I threw my hands up in the air and said, "Lord, either You've called me or You haven't! Either You're my Provider or You're not!" I was at the end of my rope. Everything was out of my control, but it was another setup from God. Speaking those words aloud caused an internal shift, bringing me to the end of myself, ready to surrender completely to the Lord and watch Him work miracles on my behalf.

REFLECTION

1. List some battles you are currently facing.

_____

_____

2. Release each of those battles to God in prayer, saying, for example, "God, I acknowledge that the battle for _____ is not mine but Yours, and I trust that You will fight it for me." Elaborate on this prayer as you feel led.

_____

_____

3. Describe, in your own words, how surrendering control to the Lord empowers you to defeat your fears.

_____

_____

Declaration

I will not fear but stay still and let God fight for me.

Day 30

FAITH IS YOUR TITLE DEED

> *Now faith is the assurance (the confirmation, the title*
> *deed) of the things [we] hope for, being the proof of things*
> *[we] do not see and the conviction of their reality [faith*
> *perceiving as real fact what is not revealed to the senses].*
> —Hebrews 11:1 AMPC

Faith is truly our title deed to the answer to every problem and provision for every need that we entrust to God. That's why we can't afford to operate in fear—by doing so, we toss out our title deed! No matter what the *facts* may say about a particular situation, it's what God says that stands forever. (See Isaiah 40:8.) Remember what happened with Abraham in regard to God's promise to make him the father of many nations:

> *Against all hope, Abraham in hope believed and so*
> *became the father of many nations, just as it had been said*
> *to him, "So shall your offspring be." Without weakening*
> *in his faith, he **faced the fact** that his body was as good*
> *as dead—since he was about a hundred years old—and*
> *that Sarah's womb was also dead. Yet **he did not waver***

*through unbelief regarding the promise of God, but was
strengthened in his faith and gave glory to God, being
fully persuaded that God had power to do what he had
promised.* (Romans 4:18–21)

The facts were stacked against him, yet Abraham maintained his belief that God would fulfill His promises to him. If we're trusting in the natural facts, we'll have plenty of opportunities to lose hope. But if we, against all hope, maintain trust in the truth of God's Word, we can believe and be blessed with all God's promises for our futures.

While we are standing in faith, it is crucial that we refuse to let the enemy mess with our minds and hearts. We should continue reading and speaking the Word concerning God's promises to us, never harboring attitudes of doubt or timidity when making requests of God. Jesus told His disciples that they would have anything they asked for in prayer, as long as they believed they had received it. (See, for example, Matthew 21:22; Mark 11:24.)

In the gospel of Mark, we read about a man who asked Jesus to heal his demon-possessed son. The man said to Jesus, *"If you can do anything, take pity on us and help us"* (Mark 9:22). Jesus responded, *"'If you can'?…Everything is possible for one who believes'"* (verse 23). There is no such thing as "if You can" with the Lord. *All* things are possible—if we only believe. When we are operating in faith, we say, "Of course, God is going to do it." "Of course, God's provision will be there, as long as we are walking in total obedience."

REFLECTION

1. What are some *facts* looming in your life?

_____

_____

2. What does God have to say about those facts, whether in His Word or through His Holy Spirit's communications to your heart?

_____

_____

3. Do you have an "*If You can*" attitude toward God? If so, pray that He would grow your faith so that you might make big requests of Him, believing without a doubt that He will come through for you.

Declaration

Everything is possible for me because I believe
he Word of God.

BREAK THE BONDAGE OF ADDICTION

Whoever conceals their sins does not prosper, but the one who confesses and renounces them finds mercy.
—Proverbs 28:13

Trusting in God's truth more than our natural circumstances does not mean that we live in a state of denial regarding reality. One of the hardest facts I ever had to face was that of my former husband's sexual addiction. For a while, I had bought his story that he hadn't visited the pornography sites I discovered on our home computer's browser history. I believed him when he told me he'd left early or come home late because of work. Breaking the cycle of addiction begins with the addict's decision to own, or acknowledge, his state of brokenness and his claiming responsibility for it. Only when the addict has accepted the fact of his brokenness can he begin to move toward finding freedom. And those who are affected by someone else's addiction must face the same reality, no longer living in denial, if they hope to find their own healing.

Coming out of denial about my husband's addiction was one of the most painful processes I have ever endured. Denial is a very effective defense mechanism that numbs the pain of reality, and when that form of anesthesia is taken away, we experience the raw pain that had formerly gone unrecognized or unacknowledged. But when we choose to face the facts about the situation—once we've allowed the Holy Spirit to remove our carnal tactics for dealing with our pain—we are free to recognize and deal with reality by the power, grace, and love of our heavenly Father. The fact may be that your spouse is struggling with an addiction, but you can be encouraged by this truth of God's Word: *"If the Son sets you free, you will be free indeed"* (John 8:36). Father God is waiting to liberate us and our loved ones from any addictions, but we must be willing to acknowledge that a problem exists.

Addicts develop their addictions under cover of darkness, which is why the evil deeds of darkness must be exposed in the light: As the light of truth illuminates these evil deeds, such as addiction, the addict can experience freedom. (See 1 John 1:5–2:1; John 3:19–21.) Once the addict escapes the shape and fear involved in keeping up an addiction, and once he has opened himself to the pain that ensues when the pain-numbing addiction has been stopped, he can begin to recognize the triggers of his addictive behavior, thereby starting the process of breaking the cycle of addiction. It's important that the addicted individual pray and ask the Holy Spirit for help in identifying his triggers. Many addicts are triggered by feelings of pain or stress.

I always say, "You gotta wantta." Someone seeking to escape the bondage of addiction must desire deliverance more than the temporary pleasure that the addictive behavior provides. They must also understand that achieving deliverance and freedom from addiction, just as from any other sin, is a process—one that even the apostle Paul struggled with. In Romans 7:15, he admitted, *"I do not understand what I do. For what I want to do I do not do, but what I hate I do."* After some further lament on still being bound by his sinful nature despite desiring to do the right thing, Paul concluded in this way: *"There is now no condemnation for those who are in Christ Jesus, because through Christ Jesus the law of the Spirit who gives life has set you free from the law of sin and death"* (Romans 8:1–2). While God's grace is not a license to sin, it extends forgiveness to those who are sincerely trying to live out their commitment to Christ.

REFLECTION

1. Read the following Scripture passages and circle any parts that stand out to you.

> *This is the message we have heard from him and declare to you: God is light; in him there is no darkness at all. If we claim to have fellowship with him and yet walk in the darkness, we lie and do not live out the truth. But if we walk in the light, as he is in the light, we have fellowship*

with one another, and the blood of Jesus, his Son, purifies us from all sin. If we claim to be without sin, we deceive ourselves and the truth is not in us. If we confess our sins, he is faithful and just and will forgive us our sins and purify us from all unrighteousness. If we claim we have not sinned, we make him out to be a liar and his word is not in us. My dear children, I write this to you so that you will not sin. But if anybody does sin, we have an advocate with the Father—Jesus Christ, the Righteous One. (1 John 1:5–2:1)

Light has come into the world, but people loved darkness instead of light because their deeds were evil. Everyone who does evil hates the light, and will not come into the light for fear that their deeds will be exposed. But whoever lives by the truth comes into the light, so that it may be seen plainly that what they have done has been done in the sight of God. (John 3:19–21)

2. How have those verses illuminated your understanding of the process of breaking the cycle of addiction? Describe this process in your own words, if it helps.

_____

_____

3. Examine your own life for any hidden, subtle addictions you may never have acknowledged before. Not all addictions are as obvious or all-consuming as sexual addiction, substance abuse, alcoholism, and so forth. Really think about any behaviors, substances, or other methods you've been counting on to numb a pain or make daily living more bearable. If you make any discoveries along these lines, go to God in prayer and ask Him to help you break the cycle of addiction, replacing those things with a relationship with Him, which is the ultimate balm for any pain.

Declaration

The light of God has purified me of all sinful behaviors and unrighteous addictions.

Day 32

RELEASING OFFENSE

*Bear with each other and forgive one another if any of
you has a grievance against someone. Forgive as the
Lord forgave you.*
—Colossians 3:13

Believe it or not, some people are addicted to bitterness and resentment. They indulge in pity parties all the time; they relish the feeling of indignation and insist on their right to feel offended. But this attitude has serious consequences. Consider this sobering exhortation from the book of Hebrews:

*Make every effort to live in peace with everyone and to
be holy; without holiness no one will see the Lord. See to
it that no one falls short of the grace of God and that* no
bitter root grows up to cause trouble and defile many.
(Hebrews 12:14–15)

Bitterness is a root that grows deeper and stronger if cultivated. Remember what I said earlier? Don't nurse it, don't rehearse it; just curse it in the name of Jesus. Don't nurse the root of bitterness by harboring it in your heart or wallowing in self-pity. Don't rehearse it by repeating over and over in your mind or out loud how much something or someone hurt you. Don't grow addicted to a *woe is me* attitude, or you'll reap devastating consequences! We must forgive others if we want to be forgiven by our heavenly Father for our own sins and wrongdoings. (See, for example, Matthew 6:12, 14–15.)

None of us has the *right* to hold on to offenses and unforgiveness, no matter how terribly someone may have hurt you. This becomes especially clear when we consider that Jesus Christ—the ultimate offended One—never once lamented His estate, even while hanging on the cross. Though He had every right to blame His accusers, and would have been justified in refusing to go through with it, He laid down His life for the sake of those who put Him to death. Talk about the opposite of bitterness! When we're tempted to feel sorry for ourselves, thinking of Jesus always puts things in perspective.

It's all too easy to focus solely on our own pain, never acknowledging or trying to imagine the painful experiences of those people we hold responsible for our own suffering. When my husband succumbed to his sexual addiction and left me and our newborn daughter, I couldn't see his own emotional distress. When my parents divorced during my childhood, I never once considered all the pain they were dealing with. Bitterness always dwells on the bad, but love lets us look for the good.

Speaking of good, we shouldn't expect to be spared offenses and hurts, even if we think we're the most pious person around. Psalm 34:19 (NKJV) reminds us, *"Many are the afflictions of the righteous."* When I first became a Christian, I thought I would never have another problem. I thought my life would be free from emotional pain because I had decided to serve Christ. It didn't take me long to realize that the opposite was true—those who follow the Lord face more than their fair share of troubles, because the devil loves to pick on us. But we can rejoice in the second part of the verse I just shared. In its entirety, Psalm 34:19 (NKJV) reads, *"Many are the afflictions of the righteous, but the LORD delivers him out of them all."* Our deliverance may not occur on this side of heaven, yet we can rest assured that our final reward will erase all memories of any offenses we have experienced in this life.

REFLECTION

1. Hebrews 12:15 warns about the root of bitterness that *"grows up to cause trouble and defile many."* Describe how this might happen and why it's important to pull up this root early and often. It may help to use a specific example from your own experience.

_____

_____

2. Do you feel surprised when you face hardships? Jesus told His followers not to be shocked when they faced the most difficult troubles, such as persecution. (See, for example, John 15:18–25.) The way we react to offense determines our destiny. Give an example of how this has been true in your own life.

_____

_____

3. Think of a time when you felt utterly wounded, rejected, or betrayed by someone. It's unlikely you stopped very long to consider how that person was feeling, or what might have motivated that person to do what he or she did. If you can do so now, put yourself in the shoes of that person and try to envision what might have been his or her experience. Then, go to God in prayer and release any remaining bitterness you've been harboring against that person.

Declaration

I refuse to cultivate the root of bitterness but will forgive freely and love liberally.

LET GO AND THE RIVER
WILL FLOW

*If only you had paid attention to my commands, your
peace would have been like a river, your well-being like
the waves of the sea.*
—Isaiah 48:18

Letting go of offenses does not come naturally to us. The
default response of our flesh is to inflict pain on those who
have wounded us. But we can't fulfill God's command to forgive unless we're prepared to let go, or release, our pain, as well
as anyone who may have contributed to it. Letting go of yesterday begins with the choice to forgive. Only when we walk
daily in forgiveness can the river of God's presence flow freely
in our lives.

Psalm 46:4 says, "*There is a river whose streams make glad
the city of God, the holy place where the Most High dwells.*" The
river mentioned in this verse symbolizes the continual out-
pouring of God's blessings, without which our souls will grow
parched and fail to thrive. As long as we refuse to yield to
the root of bitterness and the foothold of unforgiveness, the

full measure of God's blessings will flow through our lives, enabling an abundant harvest of joy, peace, and the priceless gift of God's presence. Father God has made available His peace, which surpasses all understanding (see Philippians 4:7), but we need to obey His Word by forgiving others if we want to partake of this covenant benefit.

Is the river of God's peace flowing through you today? If not, it could be that there's some junk in your river. One day while driving, I spotted what seemed to be a beautiful river. Upon closer inspection, I saw an appalling amount of junk floating in the water: broken tree limbs, discarded tires, aluminum cans, and other types of trash. Later, the Lord reminded me of the deceptively pretty river and said, "That's how My children are when they have unforgiveness in their hearts—they have junk floating in their rivers." Not only does junk in our *rivers* detract from the beauty of God's presence in our lives, but it also prevents us from flowing in the power of His presence. In order for us to extend forgiveness to others who have hurt us, we need to learn how to practice something that I like to call *soul control*.

For my first seventeen years, I was guided entirely by my soul and my flesh. Once I accepted Christ as my Lord and Savior, the Holy Spirit began to show me how I needed to be led by my spirit, submitted to the Holy Spirit's control. The soul encompasses the will, the emotions, and the natural mind. Once we come to a saving faith, our spirits are immediately restored to their proper relationship to God; our souls, on the other hand, aren't as quick to submit. The process of transferring our allegiance from our souls—what we want (our wills), what we think (our minds), and how we feel (our emotions)—to our Spirit-led spirits takes time. In the soul realm, it's all about the self; when we die to self and follow Christ, it stops being about us and starts being all about Christ.

When we get our minds, wills, and emotions in line with our spirits, nothing can stop the flow of God's blessings in our lives. Many times, the Holy Spirit has led me to do things that go against what my natural mind thinks should be done. I've had to choose to get my mind in agreement with my spirit. Praise God that the Holy Spirit leads and guides us into all truth (see John 16:13) and opens our eyes to see everything from His perspective.

REFLECTION

1. Let's check the flow of God's peace in your life. Place a check beside any of the following types of *debris* that may be dirtying your river and slowing its flow. Then, prayerfully surrender these issues to God so His Holy Spirit can work to clear up your flow and give you all-surpassing peace.

___ Unforgiveness

___ Bitterness/grudge-holding

___ Envy

____ Tendency to gossip/slander

____ Self-pity

____ Offense

____ Judgmental attitude

____ Self-righteous attitude

____ Unholy anger

____ Other: _____

2. Have you ever experienced the peace of God that passes understanding? You know you have when you reacted to a situation in a godly way—perhaps calmly and with a readiness to forgive—rather than according to your usual inclinations. If you have never experienced this type of peace personally, perhaps you have witnessed someone else exhibiting it. Either way, record your experience so that you will have something to look back on when you're in a place of unrest. Remind yourself of God's faithfulness, and pursue His peace by praying that He would reveal to you any roots of bitterness you need to remove.

_____

_____

3. Describe, in your own words, the process of mastering *soul control*. To what degree would you say your soul is submitted to your spirit?

_____

_____

Declaration

Because of soul control, I have peace like a river in my soul.

KEYS TO DIVINE PROMOTION, PART 1

Not from the east nor from the west nor from the south come promotion and lifting up. But God is the Judge! He puts down one and lifts up another.
—Psalm 75:6–7 AMPC

One of the hardest things to forgive is false accusation or slander spoken about us by someone else. There was a time when someone was spreading all kinds of vicious rumors about me, and I was tempted to verbally defend myself. But the Lord impressed upon me the importance of keeping my mouth shut and not reacting to the pervasive falsehoods. I had kept quiet for over a year when God opened the door for me to start broadcasting my evangelistic show for an hour-long segment on primetime television. He said to me, "Because you have guarded your heart and your mouth and kept silent when I told you to, I can now trust you to bring forth My Word from your mouth."

We've got to keep in mind that false accusations almost always precede supernatural promotion, as long as we keep our hearts right and forgive our accusers. Take the example of Joseph: he was falsely accused by the wife of Potiphar, his boss, and put in prison, only to find himself being promoted shortly thereafter to second in command over Egypt. (See Genesis 39:5–23; 41:1–44.) False accusations can be a platform for promotion if we pass the test by keeping our hearts right, as Joseph did. As Joseph pointed out to his brothers—his would-be murderers—when they came to Egypt seeking relief from the famine in their own country, what Satan means for evil, God can use for good, benefitting ourselves and others. (See Genesis 50:20.)

Again, it can be a real struggle to resist seeking revenge when we're falsely accused. But taking matters into our own hands only gives place to unforgiveness and bitterness, which could cause us to throw away an eternity with God. Our heavenly Father assures us that He will right all injustice, saying, *"Vengeance is Mine; I will repay"* (Romans 12:19 NKJV). Not only are we not to retaliate against those who defame us; we aren't to defend ourselves, either. *"Yet their Redeemer is strong; the LORD Almighty is his name. He will vigorously defend their cause"* (Jeremiah 50:34). If we try to defend ourselves, it's usually because of pride, which acts as a defense mechanism for insecurity. But when we are confident of our identity in Christ, it doesn't matter what anyone else thinks about us. All that matters is what God thinks.

REFLECTION

1. Have you ever been slandered or falsely accused? If so, how did it make you feel? What was your response?

_____

_____

2. What should we resist doing when we suffer injustice or false accusations, and what makes it so difficult to react the right way?

_____

_____

3. Joseph is just one biblical example of someone who had to endure slander and false accusation before he was promoted to a place of authority and blessing. Plenty of others either endured similar circumstances or had their reputations sullied, whether for the sake of serving Christ or not (though they all ended up serving Christ). For each of the following individuals, read the passages listed and then summarize their situation: what they endured and what they received in return.

♦   *Mary, the mother of Jesus* (Matthew 1:18–21; Luke 1:49)

_____

_____

♦   *The woman caught in adultery* (John 8:2–11)

_____

_____

♦   *Zacchaeus* (Luke 19:1–10)

_____

_____

♦   *Jesus Christ* (Isaiah 53:7–12; Matthew 26:57–66; Philippians 2:1–11)

_____

_____

Declaration

*Though others may speak ill of me, I'll keep silent
and let God speak for me.*

KEYS TO DIVINE PROMOTION, PART 2

*Be still before the L*ORD *and wait patiently for him; do not fret when people succeed in their ways, when they carry out their wicked schemes.*
—Psalm 37:7

When we're waiting for a promotion God has told us will happen or for the fulfillment of promises He's given us, it can be tempting to try to hurry things up. We may be inclined to *help* God out a little, just as Abraham attempted to do. Growing impatient for the son God had promised him, Abraham, with the blessing of his wife, took matters into his own hands and got his slave pregnant. (See Genesis 16:1–6.) What a mess that was! Our efforts to speed up the process can wreck things and may even delay further the fulfillment of God's plans.

I knew I was called to the ministry from a young age, but there came a time when I felt I should help God out a little, since my career wasn't taking off the way I thought it should. I'll never forget what the Lord said to me one day: "I don't need your help, just your obedience." So, I stopped *helping* and simply focused on taking one step of obedience at a time. That's when things started happening! My ministry may not have advanced as quickly as I would have preferred, but I could tell that the details were falling into place the way God planned them, and that was my biggest priority.

When God is our navigator, the route to our Promised Land is rarely the fast track. In the book of Exodus, we have this telling description of the Israelites' escape from Egypt:

> *When Pharaoh let the people go, God did not lead them on the road through the Philistine country, though that was shorter. For God said, "If they face war, they might change their minds and return to Egypt." So God led the people around by the desert road toward the Red Sea.* (Exodus 13:17–18)

God had divinely ordained the details surrounding the escape of His people from Egypt. He'd thought the whole thing through and kept the Israelites' best interests at heart. He knew the long way around would allow time for the Israelites to mature adequately to remain free from bondage.

Maybe you feel as if God has led you *"around by the desert road"* or required you to wait an excessive amount of time. I don't know about you, but I'm always on the lookout for short-cuts when I drive. But when we belong to God, we aren't in the driver's seat any longer—He is! Whether He selects the shortest route or the fastest one, the only thing He requires of us is our obedience. God does things His way so that He gets the glory. Consider this explanation He gave to Moses, who was leading the Israelites out of Egypt:

> *I will harden Pharaoh's heart, and he will pursue [you]. But I will gain glory for myself through Pharaoh and all his army, and the Egyptians will know that I am the LORD.* (Exodus 14:4)

When God is in control of our paths and promotions, it will be clear to everyone—ourselves included—that He is the One who put us in our places of blessing. He told me it was time to launch my television ministry, and, sure enough, doors started opening wide. I was a single mom having to stand in faith for diapers and baby food for my newborn daughter, but I knew that when God says it's time, I had better get ready. He needed no help from me, just my obedience.

REFLECTION

1. Have you ever tried to *help God out?* Describe your efforts and the results they produced.

_____

_____

2. The entire account of Moses leading the Israelites out of Egypt is full of excellent examples of what it means to learn to trust God and obey Him no matter what. Set aside some time to read Exodus 13:17–22 and all of chapter 14, paying attention to the places where the Israelites had to surrender their own agenda and personal preferences. Record any lasting impressions you have from this study of God's Word.

_____

_____

3. Has God ever led you *around the desert road?* Maybe He's doing that right now. Prayerfully surrender to His leading and declare your trust in His wisdom and ability to bring you to your personal Promised Land in His perfect timing.

Declaration

I will give God my obedience and not my "help."

CLOTHED IN LOVE

Clothe yourselves with compassion, kindness, humility,
gentleness and patience....Forgive as the Lord forgave
you. And over all these virtues put on love, which binds
them all together in perfect unity.
—Colossians 3:12–14

The best way to keep ourselves from harboring offense against, and seeking revenge on, any accuser is to put on the opposite attitude: love, which *"covers over a multitude of sins"* (1 Peter 4:8). It's easy enough to love others when they treat us kindly. It's another thing to love people when their faults are plain to see, especially if those faults have hurt us in some way. Learning to walk in love at all times is part of the process of becoming a mature Christian. And isn't that our ultimate goal? Spiritual maturity is the worthiest achievement we could aim for, far better than any promotion we could earn.

Once we've accepted Christ, we cease being the carnal, worldly people we used to be. Coming to salvation is a type of death—death to sin and to our carnal ways of dealing with and responding to things. If you think about it, dead people have no responses; they don't even notice when harm befalls them or bad words are spoken of them. In the words of the apostle Paul, *"You died, and your life is now hidden with Christ in God"* (Colossians 3:3). And as he put it elsewhere, *"If anyone is in Christ, the new creation has come: The old has gone, the new is here!"* (2 Corinthians 5:17).

Now we must become what we already are in Christ. We must choose to take off or *"put to death"* the old self (see Colossians 3:5) and put on, or clothe ourselves, with the new. The Lord is trying to get us dressed and ready for where we are headed, and that's a higher place in Him. We need to put on the virtues listed in Colossians 3:12–14 and wear them all day, every day. And the most important one is love. Unless we're continually clothed in love, we'll find it difficult, if not impossible, to put on the other virtues. Instead of putting on real love, some people pretend that they love. They act like they love you; they *put on* that they agree with you, only to backstab or slander you when you aren't looking. *Putting on* that we love others is not enough. We must decide to put on the garment of genuine love every day and never take it off.

As you strive to love and forgive others, please don't forget to extend love and forgiveness to yourself. I have ministered to many people who needed to forgive themselves for mistakes they had made, or thought they had made. Everyone makes choices and decisions out of a place of brokenness, to some degree, and many people classify as *disobedience* the choices they made in an earnest effort to follow God's will for their lives. Whether you disobeyed God or simply made a poor decision based on your limited, broken perspective, you need to repent and be reconciled to God—but don't forget to forgive yourself!

REFLECTION

1. Make a list of all the things in which we're supposed to *clothe ourselves* as new creations in Christ. (See Colossians 3:12–17.) Then, circle the *garments* you feel you are lacking the most. Pray that God would help you to put on those virtues and to practice them daily.

_____

_____

2. Now make a list of all the habits and attitudes we're supposed to remove from our lives. (See Colossians 3:5, 8–9). Then, draw a box around the ones you seem to have the most trouble with. Commit to noticing these behaviors and to replacing them with love, one step of obedience at a time.

_____

_____

3. Is there something for which you need to forgive yourself? It might not come to you right away, so pay attention in the coming days and weeks to anything that seems to be a lingering source of guilt. Then, release it in prayer to God and speak the following over yourself: "Because Christ has forgiven me for _____, I now forgive myself and release myself of all guilt and responsibility for it, in Jesus's name. Amen."

Declaration

*In Christ, I am free to love and forgive others—
and myself!*

ACT, DON'T REACT (OR PANIC)

Commit to the LORD whatever you do, and he will establish your plans.
—Proverbs 16:3

I waited many years to get married, only to find myself in an abusive marriage to a man who ended up having a sexual addiction. Once I discovered the alarming reality of the pit I was in, I panicked. Although I was a seasoned Christian believer who regularly strived to act out of my spirit rather than my flesh, I regressed to my carnal ways and had a full-blown panic attack in the pit. I knew then what I know now, even more fully: reacting out of our flesh when facing difficult circumstances is one of the worst things we can do because reacting engages our sinful natures, including our emotions and our natural minds. When we react out of our flesh, we affirm the power and potency of our pit. When we act out of our spirits, however, we acknowledge and affirm how much more powerful and potent is our God than the pit we're in.

A good biblical example of acting rather than reacting is recorded in 2 Chronicles 20. Jehoshaphat, king of Judah, was informed by some of his men that a vast army was coming against his people—and soon. This army intended to destroy the entire city and everyone in it. The Word tells us that while Jehoshaphat was alarmed, he did not react out of his flesh but rather out of his spirit, going straight to God with his troubles. (See 2 Chronicles 20:3–12.)

Verse 3 reads, *"Jehoshaphat resolved to inquire of the* LORD, *and he proclaimed a fast for all Judah."* In the biggest battle of his life, King Jehoshaphat sought the Lord—not his friends, his spouse, or his neighbors. He went before the Lord in fasting and prayer, and he implored those around him to do the same. He didn't react or panic, either of which would have proved a waste of time and energy. He didn't come unglued, which only would have caused his people to do the same thing. He acted, calmly inquiring of the Lord, and brought everyone together to seek the Lord's direction.

When we panic in the pit, we tend to grab hold of anything and everything we can get our hands on—whatever we can find to keep us from falling deeper into the pit. But panicking only turns those tools into shovels that dig our way down to the depths of the pit. You may have seen someone get out of a toxic relationship, only to jump immediately into another relationship more toxic than the first. Or maybe you're familiar with people who grabbed a drug or a drink in an effort to numb the pain of their pit, only to find themselves tunneling into deeper, darker pits. The key is to avoid reacting out of the flesh, or the carnal instincts, and instead to act out of a spirit that's led by the Holy Spirit.

When we panic, we try to do in the flesh what can be done only in the spirit. Again, when we react in the flesh, we usually end up digging an even deeper pit. Let's refuse to grab a shovel of our own making and instead cling faithfully to the rope of hope—the Word of God—and determine to climb out with God's help, no matter how deep our pit may seem today.

REFLECTION

1. Think of a difficult situation you are facing or have faced, and describe the way you have dealt with it, classifying each strategy as one of either *reacting* or *acting*. Which strategy has been more effective?

_____

_____

2. Have you ever grabbed hold of something you thought would help you to dig yourself out of a pit, only to find yourself digging yourself an even bigger hole? Perhaps someone you know has had this experience. Describe it.

_____

_____

3. If you're ready to stop reacting and start acting, then make the following commitment, either writing it down or speaking it aloud: "I resolve to inquire of the Lord with prayer and fasting when troubles come my way. Instead of panicking in the pit, I will calmly and confidently look to God to pull me out."

Declaration

There's no panicking in the pit when I have access to God's rope of hope.

DETERMINE TO TRUST GOD

Trust in the LORD with all your heart and lean not on your own understanding; in all your ways submit to him, and he will make your paths straight.
—Proverbs 3:5–6

King Jehoshaphat acknowledged God in the middle of his battle and looked to God for the solution to his problem. We need to recognize who God is in the midst of our battles. Sometimes, we get so caught up in acknowledging the strength of our opponent or the size of our storm that we get distracted and forget that God is in control.

Second Chronicles 20:3 tells us that Jehoshaphat *"resolved to inquire of the LORD."* To resolve means the same thing as *to determine.* The king determined to get God's opinion of his situation rather than relying on his own assessment or that of his friends and advisors. Whether we are alone in our pit or surrounded by others with their opinions circling around in our minds, we must determine to inquire of the Lord and get His opinion on things.

As a young Christian, I felt that I didn't have any gifts I could use to bring glory to God or build up His kingdom. I said to the Lord, "I can't sing, I can't play the piano. God, I don't have any gifts." Years later, the Lord said to me, "Danette, your gift is the gift of determination." I had never considered determination to be a gift, but I now realize that God gives us the talents and dispositions we need in order to fulfill His purposes for our lives and for His kingdom.

Determination can work to our disadvantage, however, if we determine to go against God. The truth is, determination will get us just about anywhere we want to go. If we are determined to pursue an outcome that isn't God's will for our lives, we can probably do so—though the journey won't be easy and the destination won't be fulfilling. But if we are determined not to quit in the pit, and if we determine to trust God, we can emerge victorious from any battle we face.

One person who learned the power of misguided determination was Jonah. The Lord directed him to go to Nineveh to deliver a message that would convict the citizens of their wickedness. (See Jonah 1:1–17.) But Jonah determined instead to travel to Tarshish—a city in the opposite direction. As Jonah traveled by boat toward Tarshish, God sent a violent storm to give Jonah an opportunity to change course. As the seas became rougher, Jonah finally admitted to the sailors that the storm was a result of his own disobedience. Once Jonah had confessed his responsibility for the storm and asked to be thrown overboard, he was supernaturally spared by being swallowed by a giant fish.

I said earlier that the storms we experience can be the result of our own disobedience, other people's disobedience, or God's desire to prune us in order to make our lives more fruitful. We need to determine to walk in obedience and, when we've traveled in a wayward direction, to determine to follow God's leading until we're back on course. When we determine to trust God and follow His leading, we can be confident of victory and freedom from any pit!

REFLECTION

1. What is your first instinct when you find yourself tossed by a storm or stuck in a pit? Number the following steps (all that apply) in the order in which you take them when troubles come.

_____ Pray

_____ Panic

_____ Ask a friend for help

_____ Talk to a pastor

_____ Cry

_____ Indulge in self-pity

_____ Brainstorm solutions

_____ Other: _____

2. Are you determined to trust God no matter what? Read the entire book of Jonah and see if it doesn't bolster your faith.

3. Have you ever determined to run away from God and chase after things that you knew to be against His will? What was the result?

_____

_____

Declaration

I'm determined to trust God and seek His opinion first in every situation.

LOOK UP, NOT AROUND YOU

*We fix our eyes not on what is seen, but on what is
unseen, since what is seen is temporary,
but what is unseen is eternal.*
—2 Corinthians 4:18

No matter what storms may come our way, we must remember to look up, get up, and never give up. By *look up*, I'm referring to the act of looking to the Lord. We shouldn't look down with our faces to the ground in discouragement, and neither should we look around at the overwhelming circumstances we're in. Rather, we must look to the Lord, who will give us the strength to get up. If we can remember to always look up and choose to get up, we are well on our way to never giving up.

While we're looking up to the Lord, we might as well pray, because prayer is a key choice to make in any pit! God's help is only a prayer away, and He delights in meeting us in our messes and showing us the way out. In fact, prayer ought to be a permanent posture, so that we're sure never to forget to pray—whether we're stuck in the deepest pit or standing on the highest mountain peak. The apostle Paul urges us, *"Rejoice always, pray continually, give thanks in all circumstances; for this is God's will for you in Christ Jesus"* (1 Thessalonians 5:16–18). That's right—we're supposed to give thanks for every circumstance, including the pit we're in!

Elsewhere, Paul writes:

> *Do not be anxious about anything, but in every situation, by prayer and petition, **with thanksgiving**, present your requests to God. And the peace of God, which transcends all understanding, will guard your hearts and your minds in Christ Jesus.* (Philippians 4:6–7)

And Paul would've known—he wrote his letter to the church in Philippi while serving a prison sentence! Jailed for his faith, he could nevertheless say, *"Rejoice in the Lord always. I will say it again: Rejoice!"* (Philippians 4:4). Because of his stance of continual prayer and nonstop focus on the Lord, Paul viewed his imprisonment as an opportunity to evangelize the prison staff (see Philippians 1:12–14), trusted that his experience would turn out for his ultimate good (see verse 19), and proclaimed that he didn't fear dying for the sake of the gospel (see verses 20–24). What a remarkable example of living by faith and maintaining the proper perspective in the pit.

It was while he was trapped in the belly of a big fish that Jonah finally prayed, repenting of his waywardness and proclaiming his trust that God would deliver him from his pit.

(See Jonah 2:1–9.) Immediately following that prayer, God commanded the fish to spit Jonah out onto dry land, saving his life. (See verse 10.) And this time, when the Lord directed Jonah to go to Nineveh with a message for the people, Jonah went without delay. (See Jonah 3:1–3.)

I won't promise that prayer is a guarantee of immediate delivery from your pit. Sometimes, our pits are meant to teach us how to pray, and the process may take a while. There's nothing like a pit to get you praying. I can honestly say that I have had some of my best, most fruitful prayer times while stuck in a pit. The key is to pray at all times, especially in the pit, looking up instead of down or all around. When you pray, God is there with you in the pit, and His presence is better than even the most dramatic deliverance.

REFLECTION

1. Would you say that you *pray continually*? If the thought of praying long, drawn-out prayers first thing in the morning or at bedtime overwhelms you, try to make a habit of praying throughout the day, keeping up a quiet conversation with God in your spirit. This practice takes time to turn into a habit, but it's one of the best ways you can cultivate intimacy with the Lord and stay attuned to the gentle leading of His Spirit.

2. Set aside a time to read the entire book of Philippians; don't worry, it's only four chapters long. Jot down, and even try

to memorize, any of the verses that stand out to you as particularly encouraging. This incredible testimony of the apostle Paul is sure to alter your perspective of your own pits and to prove to you how transformative a rock-solid trust in God can be.

_____

_____

3. The apostle Paul writes, *"Rejoice in the Lord always. I will say it again: Rejoice!"* (Philippians 4:4). A tall order, but it becomes feasible when you focus on fulfilling it. The next time you're tempted to mope and wallow in self-pity, describe your circumstances, and then identify something positive that you can rejoice in nonetheless. I've left several blanks so that you can practice this exercise on multiple occasions—perhaps within the same day!

Negative Circumstance	Rejoice Because...
_____	_____
_____	_____
_____	_____
_____	_____
_____	_____

Declaration

I will rejoice continually in the God who is with me in the pit.

Day 40

FOCUS ON THE FINISH LINE

Forgetting what is behind and straining toward what is ahead, I press on toward the goal to win the prize for which God has called me heavenward in Christ Jesus.
—Philippians 3:13–14

We can never be defeated if we never quit. Victory is sure when we know who we are and Whose we are! God is so wise in showing us the finish line—where we're ultimately headed—so we will be encouraged to never give up in the middle of the race. At the starting line, and even during the course, we don't know what we'll face; but we do know the finish line, the destination God has shown us. If we remain focused on the finish line, we won't fall for the distractions and discouragement we encounter as we run the race.

Our goal should be that of the apostle Paul when he said, *"I consider my life worth nothing to me; my only aim to finish the race and complete the task the Lord Jesus has given me—the task of testifying to the good news of God's grace"* (Acts 20:24). Victory consists of fulfilling all that the Lord has created us to do, thereby *finishing the race*—and the ultimate victory is found in an eternity spent with the Lord. If the finish line in this life is the completion of our purpose and call, then the sooner we get an understanding of that finish line, the better. We may not receive a clear picture of exactly where we're headed, but God will reveal to us, in His perfect timing, what it is that He has called us to do.

God revealed Joseph's *finish line* in a dream when Joseph was young. (See Genesis 37:5–9.) Joseph saw his finish line long before even starting the race—and it was a good thing, too, because the pits Joseph would encounter along the way would present plenty of temptations to give up. No, Joseph's dream didn't include his getting sold into slavery by his own brothers (see Genesis 37:26–33); working faithfully as a servant for a leader in Egypt, only to find himself thrown in prison when that leader's wife wrongly accused him (see Genesis 39:2–20); or being forgotten by a man who promised to try to help him get out of prison (see Genesis 40). Yet, in all these things, Joseph prospered because the Lord was with him and gave him success in everything he did. (See Genesis 39:3, 23.)

Through every setback, Joseph kept his focus on the finish line. As a result, he was not derailed from his God-directed course. He knew that God was strategically positioning him and preparing him for his place in the palace—his finish line. At God's appointed time, Joseph was promoted to a place of authority over all the land of Egypt because he had maintained a right heart attitude and upheld his godly character.

(See Genesis 41.) And God prepares *us* for our own finish lines—for the fulfillment of our purposes—as we run the race of life. We must grow in wisdom, discernment, and godly character before we reach the finish line. Everything that God has shown you will come to pass, as long as you refuse to quit in the pit and keep focusing on the finish line. Your pit isn't permanent—it's just a *pit stop* on your path to the palace!

Even if you don't receive a revelation of your finish line, keep in mind that the ultimate destination is a heavenly eternity with our Lord and Savior. No matter what, we need to "[fix] *our eyes on Jesus, the pioneer and perfecter of faith*" (Hebrews 12:2). Peter walked on water at Jesus's command—until he moved his gaze from Jesus to the wind and waves, at which point he began to sink. (See Matthew 14:22–32.) The best, surest finish line to focus on is Christ Himself!

REFLECTION

1. Has God showed you your *finish line*—your call and purpose? Write down any revelations He's given you along these lines, and pray that He would refine this picture so that you might focus on the finish line and overcome distractions.

_____

_____

2. What definition of *victory* do you live by? Is it the same as Paul's definition in Acts 20:24? If not, you may need to reorient your understanding of this concept.

3. What godly character traits and attributes is the Lord growing in you today? In which areas do you need growth?

_____

_____

Declaration

I fix my eyes on the finish line—the fulfillment of God's will for me.

DON'T QUIT IN THE PIT

Therefore we do not lose heart. Though outwardly we are wasting away, yet inwardly we are being renewed day by day. For our light and momentary troubles are achieving for us an eternal glory that far outweighs them all.
—2 Corinthians 4:16–17

Like Joseph did, I knew from a young age where I was headed in the Lord. However, I encountered many unexpected circumstances and unforeseen setbacks—from getting divorced to becoming a single parent to struggling to make ends meet—all of which made the prospect of quitting seem highly desirable, if not inevitable. Not only did I feel like quitting in my pit, but there were plenty of people telling me my ministry was over. Hearing that message of negativity was like being trapped at the bottom of a pit while everyone around me shoveled dirt on my head.

In the midst of these painful pits, God kept telling me to focus on the finish line. He pointed to the example of Joseph to encourage me, and He reassured me that nothing could disqualify me from His call on my life—nothing, that is, except for my own choices. No one else's choices could cause me to miss out on all He had in store for me. As long as I kept my heart free from bitterness and unforgiveness, and as long as I chose to obey God's leading one step at a time, I felt confident that God would see me out of every pit.

I want to encourage you in the same way today. Never quit in the pit! Your heart attitude and your choices are the only things that could possibly disqualify you from reaching the finish line and finding victory in Jesus. Just determine to follow the leading of the Holy Spirit—including any seemingly illogical instructions He gives—and you will enter into the Promised Land of blessings God has for you.

Your circumstances may change, your income may change, and your mailing address may change, but God's call on your life hasn't changed, and neither has the One who placed that call in the first place. God is the same yesterday, today, and forever. (See Hebrews 13:8.) He is still on His throne, and always will be, with Jesus seated at His right hand, interceding for you and me. (See Romans 8:34.)

Maybe you have never sought God concerning His will for your life. Maybe you've never fully surrendered to Him as Lord and Savior. Today can be your day to do so! Don't wait to get thrown into a pit before seeking God. However, if you find yourself in a pit right now, there's no better place from which to call on the name of the Lord. Remember, *"Everyone who calls on the name of the Lord will be saved"* (Joel 2:32). He's just waiting for you to call on His name. So don't quit in the pit, but reach for the rope of hope and trust God to pull you out!

REFLECTION

1. Have you ever been really tempted to quit in the pit? What was it that brought you out? (Or maybe you did quit and you're still in that pit. If that's the case, seek the Lord in prayer, and also seek godly counsel for help.)

_____

_____

2. Did you realize before reading today's entry that nothing besides your attitude and choices can disqualify you from fulfilling God's call on your life? List any places where you tend to direct blame for your current position, from people to circumstances to personal traits. Then, cross them out to symbolize their being *off the hook* for where you are right now.

_____

_____

3. Hebrews 13:8 reads, *"Jesus Christ is the same yesterday and today and forever."* Isn't it staggering to grasp the fact that the same God who created Adam and Eve, raised up Moses, blessed Abraham, rescued Jonah, promoted Joseph,

and delivered Paul is available to help us today? Back up a few chapters in Hebrews to read all of chapter 11, commonly called the "Hall of Faith." Each of the people mentioned there called on the same God who loves and cares for you today. Let that soak in!

Declaration

I refuse to quit in the pit!

Day 42

REBUILD THE WALLS

Carry each other's burdens, and in this way
you will fulfill the law of Christ.
—Galatians 6:2

Once God has gotten you out of your pit, your journey is far from over. When you're free from the pit—or, sometimes, even while you're still in the pit—God will use you to help others out of their own pits. Just like Nehemiah, cupbearer to King Artaxerxes, who left home to help the Israelites out of their pit of despair by leading the effort to rebuild the wall around Jerusalem (see Nehemiah 2:1–6), we need to make ourselves available for God to use the brokenness of our experience in rebuilding the broken walls in others' lives. You can free others from their pits and, like Nehemiah, restore the ruins of their lives, equipping them to possess God's promises of blessing for them.

Nehemiah had a heart for his people because he felt the same desire to see the wall of Jerusalem restored. When a situation hits home with us, we can cultivate hearts of compassion that compel us to reach out and help other people who are hurting as we have hurt. My most powerful and effective teachings have come from the difficult experiences I've been through. People usually need to believe we have a heart for them—that we feel their pain and have been in their shoes—before they allow us to help them rebuild their broken-down walls.

As Nehemiah sought to rebuild the wall of Jerusalem, he needed some big favors from the king, including time off from work and multiple letters of reference. And because the hand of God was on Nehemiah, the king went above and beyond granting Nehemiah's requests. (See Nehemiah 2:7–8.) When you have the favor of God, you can't help but have the favor of man. And if God understands that you have a heart for helping His people, He will surely commission you to help them rebuild the broken areas of their lives. It may seem like a daunting task, but if the King of Kings commissions you, then you know you'll have everything you need.

Of course, Nehemiah's efforts were not without challenges, perhaps the most annoying of which were the men who opposed his plan and plotted to put a stop to it. (See Nehemiah 4:1–3, 7–9, 11.) These men threatened violence in an effort to distract Nehemiah and the other laborers from their work. When we're on board with the Lord's rebuilding process and we reach out to help others, Satan doesn't take it sitting down. He tries to get us so caught up with our own troubles that we don't have the time or energy to reach out and

assist our brothers and sisters. That's one reason it's so important to keep our eyes off ourselves. If we will keep our focus on
God and maintain hearts of compassion for others, we keep
ourselves available to help others rebuild. After all, no matter
how badly we are hurting, there is always someone else whose
pain is worse than ours.

I'm not saying you should dismiss or deny your pain, or
that you shouldn't forgo a time of healing for yourself. I'm
saying only that you shouldn't pitch a tent and camp out in
your pain. Get up out of your own mess and seed your need
by reaching out to someone who's hurting even more than you
are. Making yourself available in this way will ensure you don't
get trapped at any pity parties!

If we stay available to God, there's no limit to what He can
and will do through us. If I had not stayed available to God
during the storms of my life, I wouldn't have written this book,
and I would have missed out on the joy of years spent ministering to millions of people through television and multiple
thousands through the various outreaches of my ministry.

Nehemiah encouraged the laborers who feared attack by
their opponents with these words: *"Don't be afraid of them.
Remember the Lord, who is great and awesome.… Our God will
fight for us!"* (Nehemiah 4:14, 20). Remember the Lord, who
is great and awesome! Remember what He's done for you—
the losses restored, the walls rebuilt—and ready yourself to be
used by Him to help others have that same testimony.

REFLECTION

1. Has anyone ever used his or her experience with struggles to help you with a trouble of your own? Describe.

_____

_____

2. What are some of the hardships you have dealt with, or are now dealing with, that might make you available and qualified for God to use in ministering help to others?

_____

_____

3. Is there anyone you know who could benefit from hearing your testimony of God's faithfulness? Prayerfully consider this question and whether the time is right to share your witness.

Declaration

*I will make myself available for God to use
in rebuilding others' walls.*

PERSEVERE WITH PATIENCE

*Consider it pure joy, my brothers and sisters, whenever
you face trials of many kinds, because you know that
the testing of your faith produces perseverance. Let
perseverance finish its work so that you may be mature
and complete, not lacking anything.*
—James 1:2–4

Once I had learned the importance of making myself
available for the Lord to use in rebuilding the walls in others'
lives, I advanced to the process of preparing to cross over to
the next level, both in my relationship with God and in my
ministry. Having made up my mind that I would be ready and
willing to tackle whatever need came my way, I wanted to get
the show on the road! I was looking for a fast-forward button
for myself and my ministry. That's when the Lord said to me,
"Relax. You're in process."

Relaxing has never come naturally to me. I soon discovered that the process God had in mind would take time and
wouldn't be altogether pleasant. I was going to have to face

"trials of many kinds"—too many to fit in one book! But it is only after perseverance *finishes its work* in our lives that we will be mature and complete in the Lord, ready to climb out of our pits with His help and to reach out a hand to assist others. To *persevere* means "to persist in a state, enterprise, or undertaking in spite of counterinfluences, opposition, or discouragement." Persevering is the essence of never quitting or giving up.

Unless we become mature and complete by practicing perseverance in the trials we face, we will be lacking in many areas and won't be much help to ourselves, let alone anyone else. But if we stick it out while perseverance finishes its work, we won't lack anything. At that point, we will be available and ready for God to use us in big ways!

If you don't think God can use you in big ways, just remember that throughout the Bible, God almost always did big things with limited resources, through people who were lacking in might and ability. He rarely did big things using plentiful resources or powerful people. God used a tiny shepherd boy to slay a giant with a sling and a stone, an enemy whom the entire Israelite army had been too afraid to face. (See 1 Samuel 17:4–50). God empowered an elderly man to raise his staff and part the waters of the Red Sea so that the Israelites could cross on dry land. (See Exodus 14.) He fed 5,000 men—plus whatever number of women and children were present—with just five loaves of bread and two fish. (See Matthew 14:19–21.) And these are just a few examples!

In the feeding of the five thousand, Jesus started with what He had, looked up to heaven, gave thanks, and took a step of faith before the food multiplied miraculously. When we step out in faith and start doing what we know God has called us to do, in spite of scant resources or other limitations, provision will always be there. Too often, people don't accomplish great things for God because they keep looking at what they *don't* have. We don't need ample resources to do great things for God. When God is in the mix, our small resources are enough because He's the God of more than enough. When we have ample resources, we're less likely to rely on our heavenly Father. Stop focusing on what you don't have and start using what you do have, for the glory of God.

REFLECTION

1. Have you ever been impatient for God to use you in some big way? Perhaps that's how you feel right now. Could it be that you're in process—that God is trying to do a work in you to prepare you for the work He has for you to do? Prayerfully consider this, and record any insights the Lord gives to you.

_____

_____

2. Which life events have most tested and strengthened your perseverance? Think about and list them here, taking note of the nature of those events—whether they were pleasant circumstances or challenging ones.

_____

_____

3. What *limitations* have been keeping you from stepping out in faith and following God's leading? Pray that God would help you to trust Him and act in spite of these perceived limitations.

Declaration

My God will make provision in whatever
He has called me to do.

LEAD OTHERS INTO THE LAND

You need to persevere so that when you have done the
will of God, you will receive what he has promised.
—Hebrews 10:36

Our goal should be to draw other people into relationship with God and then to help those people climb to the next level in Him. Just as He instructed Joshua to get the Israelites packed and ready to take possession of the land He had promised them (see Joshua 1:1–11), God wants us to lead those around us out of the pit and into the possession of their Promised Land.

We don't climb out of the pit and take possession of the land by sitting back and idly twiddling our thumbs. We don't advance to the next level in God by lying on the couch watching TV. We advance by force, and that requires some elbow grease on our part. The continual refrain of God's message to Joshua was *"be strong and courageous"*—He made that exhortation three times in the span of a few verses: Joshua 1:6, 7, and

9. In verse 7, God emphasizes, *"Be strong and **very** courageous."* And He's saying the same thing to us today.

Only forceful men and women will lay hold of all that God has for them—those willing to fight mightily against the kingdom of darkness and to advance, with force, the kingdom of God. (See Matthew 11:12.) Possessing anything entails taking a step of faith—a strong, courageous step of faith.

The Lord said to Joshua, *"I will give you every place where you set your foot, as I promised Moses"* (Joshua 1:3). In order to possess the places he'd been promised, Joshua needed to *set his foot,* or take an upward step of faith toward the next level. Just a few verses later, God told Joshua *why* he would need to be strong and courageous: *"…because you will lead these people to inherit the land I swore to their ancestors to give them"* (Joshua 1:6).

I can imagine that one of Joshua's first thoughts might have been, *Who, me?* That's often how we respond when God tells us He's going to use us for something. Yet each of us is called to be a leader in some way. A mother is called to lead her children. An employee at any level is called to lead his or her coworkers by example. And all of us are called to lead others to Christ.

Weeping may endure for a night, but joy comes in the morning. (See Psalm 30:5.) No matter how severe the storm, no matter how deep the pit, and no matter how long the night, the sun will shine again. If we remain obedient to our heavenly Father, He not only pulls us out of the pit and into the sunshine but also causes His Son to shine through us, lighting the way for others.

Don't allow yourself to be intimidated or discouraged, but determine to climb to the next level in God, trusting Him to lead you as you lead others. Once you've escaped your own pit and ascended the peak, make sure you remember to reach out and give a hand to others who are seeking escape from their own pits. Then you will glorify God together, and glory in His faithfulness!

REFLECTION

1. Is God telling you to be strong and courageous? The best fuel for your courage consists in prayer and Bible study. Make sure you're setting aside time with the Lord and reading His Word on a regular basis.

_____

_____

2. How are you a leader? Don't think about the usual roles of leaders and followers; really consider those who are watching you and are subject to your influence. Pray that God would show you how to walk in such a way that you lead those people to Him.

_____

_____

3. Who do you know who's in a pit and needs help getting out? Pray for wisdom regarding how God might use you to lead that person out of the pit and toward the Promised Land in God.

Declaration

I will lead the way for others to climb out of their pits and know Christ.

Day 45

GET REAL AND DEAL

Where no wise guidance is, the people fall, but in the
multitude of counselors there is safety.
—Proverbs 11:14 AMPC

Many people spend an entire lifetime wandering like the children of Israel in the wilderness, ultimately quitting in the pit before even coming close to crossing over into the fulfillment of God's promises to them. Let's not be counted in that category! When we remember that tough times don't last, but tough people do, we can get real and deal, successfully, with any pit we face. We can be *"more than conquerors"* (Romans 8:37) and overcome any trial we encounter.

The basic requirement for getting out of any pit is to *get real* and endure the painful process of dropping any denial we've been living with. We must face the facts about our circumstances, keeping in mind that the truth of God always prevails. The reason people remain in denial is usually that the process of dealing with the truth about one's circumstances can cause a great deal of emotional pain and anguish. But as we remind ourselves daily of the truth of God's Word, we can rely on God's supernatural strength to get real and deal.

After getting real by facing our situation head-on, we need to *deal* with the problem. One key to dealing with our personal pits is knowing what God's Word says about us and our situations. That foundational knowledge equips us with a mindset to maintain faith in the face of troubles. Another completely valid course of action is to seek sound Christian counseling. Godly counselors have been a lifeline to me, helping me navigate through the murky waters of low self-esteem, marital problems, single parenthood, and many other pits.

It was many years ago that I first sought professional Christian counseling, and I will admit that it isn't always easy to find a professional, licensed Christian counselor you can trust. But if you maintain a steady diet of the Word of God, cultivating a strong relationship with the Lord, then you will have enough discernment to recognize whether your counselor is acting as a faithful mouthpiece of the Lord.

Just yesterday, I spoke with a couple who had been married nine years and were about to throw in the towel. They were at their wits' end. I asked the husband whether they had tried Christian counseling. He told me that they had attended a couple of sessions but had decided to stop going. Here's what I told him: attending a counseling session for an issue you need to deal with is like having a splinter removed from your hand. It's painful and it's raw, but it's coming out of denial in the most powerful way.

There are endless excuses a person can make to justify giving up on counseling: not enough money, inadequate childcare, lack of time, and so forth. But anyone who desires healing must get real and deal. No matter what's required, the pain and sacrifice are well worth getting you out of your pit in a healthy, productive way.

Anything worth having is worth fighting for, including peace, joy, fulfillment, and contentment; a strong marriage; well-adjusted children; healthy relationships; and a promising future. Remember, tough times don't last, but tough people do. Determine to do whatever God calls you to do to cross over into all of God's promises for you!

REFLECTION

1. Are you living in a state of denial? Prayerfully consider whether there is anything about which you need to *get real* in order to begin the process of climbing out of your pit.

2. Maybe you've already *gotten real* and have an authentic understanding of just what it is you need to deal with. Are you ready to start dealing? Pray that God would reveal to you the first steps you ought to take, and whether seeking the help of a certified Christian counselor might benefit you.

3. What is it you're fighting for today? Write it down below, then proclaim out loud that you will continue to fight,

trusting God for victory. Make this declaration every day for as long as it takes to see victory!

I'm fighting for _____. I believe God will give me ultimate victory, and I trust Him to lead me every step of the way.

Declaration

The life God has planned for me is worth fighting for!

ABOUT THE AUTHOR

Danette Crawford is a powerful speaker, author, TV host, and international evangelist with a refreshing message of hope and encouragement. The founder and president of Danette Crawford Ministries, she earned a master's degree in counseling from Regent University.

Danette Crawford Ministries' outreach arm, Joy Ministries Evangelistic Association, organizes inner-city work with more than twenty-two different compassion programs dedicated to sustainable aid through education and mentoring, assistance for at-risk youth and low-income families, and programs for single mothers, including Cars for Moms, Back to Work programs, and the Father's House.

Danette's television program, *Hope for Today with Danette Crawford*, is broadcast weekly into over 250 million homes, airing on ABC, CBS, TBN, WHT, CTN, NRB, Goodlife45, Atlanta 57, and Dove Network.

Danette is the author of several books, including *Don't Quit in the Pit; Limitless Thinking, Limitless Living; God, You've Got Mail;* and *Standard Setters*. In everything she does, her goal is to change lives and show others that they can overcome any difficulty that comes their way.

For more information, visit www.DanetteCrawford.com.